SOVIET
MILITARY
POWER
1984

The United States Government has not recognized the incorporation of Estonia, Latvia and Lithuania into the Soviet Union. Other boundary representations on the maps in *Soviet Military Power 1984* are not necessarily authoritative.

The illustrations of Soviet weapons systems introducing each chapter and elsewhere are derived from various US sources; while not precise in every detail, they are as authentic as possible.

CONTENTS

PREFACE

"I made two promises to the American people about peace
and security: I promised to restore our neglected defenses in
order to strengthen and preserve the peace, and I promised to
pursue reliable agreements to reduce nuclear weapons. Both
these promises are being kept."

Ronald Reagan
March 1983

For almost 40 years, the United States has remained steadfastly committed to deterrence and arms reductions. As we enter the mid-1980s, our dual goals are to enhance the strategic stability contributing to the security of the United States and our Allies and to obtain genuine and verifiable reductions to equal levels in nuclear weapons so as to lessen the risk of a war that neither side could win. In pursuing these goals, we must continue to assess the threat posed by the growing size and capabilities of the Soviet Union's Armed Forces. That assessment reveals:

• The USSR has greatly increased its offensive military capability and has significantly enhanced its ability to conduct military operations worldwide.

• The Soviet build-up is made possible by a national policy that has consistently made military materiel production its highest economic priority.

Underlying Soviet military power is a vast and complex industrial, mobilization and logistics support system designed to focus the resources of the Soviet State on the capability to wage war. For decades, Soviet industry has manufactured a broad spectrum of weaponry and military support equipment in staggering quantities—production levels achieved by extremely large investments of money, raw materials and manpower. Moreover, the Soviet leadership places the highest priority on the utilization of science and technology for military purposes, and this, together with exploitation of Western technology, has sharply eroded the qualitative edge that the West had used to balance the Soviet lead in numbers of weapons and men.

The Soviet Union has in place a national mobilization system that penetrates every sector of Soviet life. This includes a logistics system designed to draw upon all classes of consumable supplies and war reserve equipment available in the USSR, as well as transport, repair and construction units. It includes a manpower pool to augment the active-duty Armed Forces and to replace losses.

The Soviets have undertaken extensive logistics preparations both in designated theaters of military operations throughout the Soviet Union and beyond Soviet borders. In Eastern Europe, the Western USSR and the Soviet Far East, priority has been given to prestocking critical ammunition and military fuel stocks. In Eastern Europe, Soviet logistics depots contain not only fuel and ammunition but also a great tonnage of military river-crossing equipment and tactical oil pipeline for which there can be no defensive justification.

Soviet Military Power 1984 provides a detailed report on the structure of the Soviet military and its pervasive role, as assigned by the Soviet leadership, in Soviet society—and how that translates directly into the increasing threat posed by the USSR's Armed Forces.

Building on the data provided in the First and Second Editions, *Soviet Military Power 1984* examines key developments in the continuing upgrade of the USSR's Armed Forces.

• Modernization of the fourth-generation SS-18 and SS-19 ICBMs nears an end, while the USSR proceeds with the testing of the fifth-generation SS-X-24 and SS-X-25 ICBMs. There are no security requirements for the development of so large a quantity of strategic nuclear offensive weapons.

• The 25,000-ton TYPHOON-Class strategic ballistic missile submarine, which in 1983 was conducting test firings of its SS-N-20 missiles, is now fully operational. And now, another new SLBM, the SS-NX-23, is being tested.

• The Soviet Union has three long-range, land-attack nuclear-armed cruise missiles nearly deployed—the sea-launched SS-NX-21, the aircraft-launched AS-X-15 and the ground-launched SSC-X-4—and it is pressing ahead with the development of more advanced strategic cruise missiles.

• The Soviets now have three manned strategic bombers in development or production. In addition to the new BLACKJACK long-range strategic bomber and the BACKFIRE bomber, the USSR has reopened production lines for the BEAR bomber and is producing a new BEAR H variant assessed to be the initial carrier for the AS-X-15 cruise missile.

• The Soviets have continued to field additional mobile SS-20 launchers, each with a three-warhead missile and reload. In 1981, *Soviet Military Power* reported 250 launchers; in 1983, the total had risen to 330 launchers and now the total is 378 launchers. Construction of new SS-20 facilities in the Western USSR has resumed, even though 243 SS-20 missiles with 729 warheads and an equal number for refire are already in place opposite NATO.

• New MiG-29/FULCRUM twin-engine fighter interceptors are now being introduced into Soviet air forces, greatly increasing offensive air capabilities. Additionally, the Su-27/FLANKER is nearing deployment.

• Fast-paced development continues in the Soviet space shuttle program, which will further increase the flexibility and capability of the USSR's essentially military manned and unmanned space systems.

• The USSR continues a great investment in strategic and tactical defenses—with across-the-board upgrading of Soviet air, sea, land and missile defense forces.

This report documents the continuing Soviet buildup. To cite an additional example—1983 saw the launching of two new classes of nuclear attack submarines, increasing to eight the total number of classes of Soviet submarines now in production and contributing to an increasingly capable submarine fleet now nearing 400 units.

Soviet Military Power 1984 includes NATO-Warsaw Pact comparisons and data on US and Allied forces to place Soviet force developments in clear perspective. It is useful to remind ourselves that the United States, as a democracy, regularly makes available full and public reports on US force developments in such publications as my *Annual Report* and the *Military Posture* by the Organization of the Joint Chiefs of Staff. The USSR makes no such reports available on Soviet Forces.

We do see, however, how they are using those forces. The shooting down of the Korean civilian airliner, with the loss of 269 innocent lives, reminds us of the USSR's willingness to use military force. The store of Soviet weapons discovered in Grenada reminds us of the USSR's willingness to extend its military influence. There are other reminders. Since invading Afghanistan 4 years ago, the USSR has established bases within striking distance of the Persian Gulf oil fields. The Soviets continue to deliver a growing arsenal of weapons to Syria, Libya, Cuba and Nicaragua. Since 1980, the number of Soviet personnel in Syria has grown from 2,000 to 7,000; and now, the Soviet military presence there is underscored by the appearance of well-equipped air defense units. The USSR's Cuban proxies in Angola and Ethiopia, and Soviet support to Vietnamese forces in Kampuchea, further dramatize growing Soviet military involvement throughout the world.

A full and clear appreciation of the threat we face provides the basis and the rationale for our defense program—a program designed to maintain our course on the two parallel paths to peace. The Soviets have not made that easy for us. Deterrence, so essential to our survival, will remain a difficult strategy. Indeed, it is a paradox of deterrence that the longer it succeeds the less necessary it appears. In arms negotiations, the USSR will repeatedly test our resolve before responding constructively.

The United States and its Allies have made progress toward restoring the military balance. We can achieve our twin goals. But to succeed, we must sustain not only our unity of purpose as a nation, but also our determination to complete the task we have begun—to restore the strength necessary to maintain peace with freedom.

Caspar W. Weinberger
Secretary of Defense

April 1984

The Soviet Military Establishment

The role played by the Communist Party of the Soviet Union (CPSU) is central to the operations of the Soviet military establishment and to the continuing growth and modernization of Soviet military power. The CPSU controls military concepts, resources and senior personnel. The top Party leadership establishes military doctrine and approves Soviet military strategy. The Defense Council, dominated by the Party leadership, controls the defense budget and makes the decisions to develop and deploy all major weapon systems. Senior officers are selected from a Central Committee list, and all major organizational changes in the Soviet military are approved by the Defense Council. Compliance with Party control of the Soviet military establishment is exercised by the Central Committee's uniformed political officers through the regular Party organization in the Armed Forces.

Military Command Structure

The CPSU General Secretary's chairmanship of the Defense Council underscores the Party's dominance over the entire command structure of the Soviet Armed Forces. Officially described by the Soviets as part of the government structure, the USSR Defense Council is, in reality, the senior and most critical Party decisionmaking body for all aspects of national security policy. In peacetime, its power over the Armed Forces is exercised directly through the Ministry of Defense and the Soviet General Staff. The Defense Council's authority covers virtually all major

The SS-X-25 Intercontinental Ballistic Missile, one of two new fifth generation ICBMs being tested from the Plesetsk rangehead, is likely designed for mobile deployment, increasing Soviet ICBM force survivability and further enhancing the capabilities of Soviet military power.

military issues. The Defense Council structure encompasses the senior cadre of Soviet political, military and economic leadership, which, from the Soviet perspective, is an essential prerequisite for the rapid and effective development of Soviet military power.

The primary administrative organ of the peacetime military command structure is the Ministry of Defense. It is responsible for directing the development of the Armed Forces of the Soviet Union. The top level of authority in the Ministry consists of Marshal D.F. Ustinov, three First Deputies and 11 Deputy Ministers, the highest ranking of whom is the Chief of the General Staff, Marshal N.V. Ogarkov. In addition to the Deputies, who are Commanders-in-Chief of the five services, other ministers and chiefs are responsible for a broad range of administrative and technological matters, such as civil defense, rear services, military construction, armaments and personnel. Ustinov serves as the principal link between the military and the Party-State apparatus. Chief of the General Staff Ogarkov is the military figure who heads the unified military establishment and the chiefs of the five services.

The General Staff also plays an important role at the national level by providing the most authoritative information to the Defense Council. It is the most important link between the political leadership and the Armed Forces themselves. Because the General Staff exercises actual operational control over the Armed Forces, it has the responsibility for translating strategy, doctrine and policy into action.

These command responsibilities make Marshal Ogarkov the single most important individual in the day-to-day operations of the Armed Forces. He is assisted by a professional military staff characterized as the "brain of the Army." The General Staff organization is designed to provide a basic command structure for controlling the Soviet Armed Forces.

Nationally, the Soviet Union is organized into 16 military districts, which serve as a geographical framework for military-administrative purposes. These districts are territorial extensions of the Ministry of Defense, encompassing various local military units and organizations and military-educational institutions. The main functions served by the districts are training and mobilization. The districts also act as agents for the coordination and implementation of civil defense measures. Each is headed by a district commander who is assisted by a military council and a district staff.

The Soviets' peacetime command structure serves two primary purposes: it provides Party leaders with the means for building modern military forces, and provides the basic framework for their planned wartime military command structure. The Soviets attach great importance to their ability to effect a rapid transition from peace to war with a minimal disruption of their command structure. Consequently, during wartime, the Soviets would create a command structure derived directly from their peacetime command structure.

The STAVKA (Headquarters) of the Supreme High Command (or VGK) would exercise control of an actual military effort in wartime. The Supreme Commander-in-Chief would serve as chairman of the STAVKA, since the organization is subordinate to the Wartime Defense Council. STAVKA members would include civil and military authorities, with support from the General Staff.

In war, the Supreme High Command would control the Armed Forces through intermediate level commands established in the Theater of Military Operations (TVD), that particular territory within whose limits a portion of the armed forces of a country or coalition operates in wartime. The control of the military forces (fronts, armies and fleets) in each of the Theaters would come under the authority of a TVD commander, who, in turn, would be subordinate to the General Staff and Supreme High Command.

Within the Soviet Union itself, the military districts provide the VGK with an administrative structure for controlling a range of domestic wartime functions. In that regard, the military districts would concentrate on the mobilization of additional manpower and resources. They would implement civil defense and air defense measures designed to limit disruption of the rear. District commanders would also follow Defense Council and Supreme High Command directives on matters concerning the conduct of the war in their particular area. District commanders could exercise their own authority under prearranged conditions.

The Soviets, thus, have in place a military command structure, dominated and controll-

Stavka of the Soviet Supreme High Command

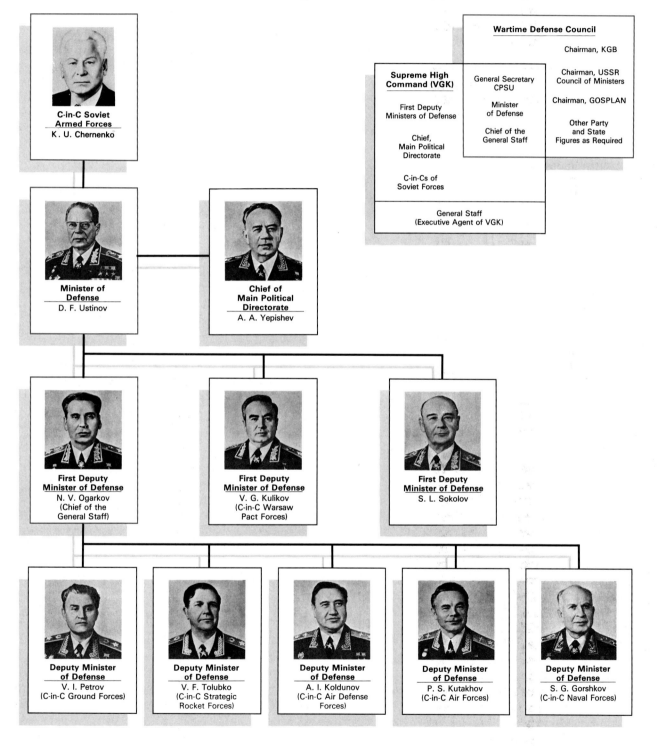

C-in-C Soviet Armed Forces
K. U. Chernenko

Minister of Defense
D. F. Ustinov

Chief of Main Political Directorate
A. A. Yepishev

First Deputy Minister of Defense
N. V. Ogarkov
(Chief of the General Staff)

First Deputy Minister of Defense
V. G. Kulikov
(C-in-C Warsaw Pact Forces)

First Deputy Minister of Defense
S. L. Sokolov

Deputy Minister of Defense
V. I. Petrov
(C-in-C Ground Forces)

Deputy Minister of Defense
V. F. Tolubko
(C-in-C Strategic Rocket Forces)

Deputy Minister of Defense
A. I. Koldunov
(C-in-C Air Defense Forces)

Deputy Minister of Defense
P. S. Kutakhov
(C-in-C Air Forces)

Deputy Minister of Defense
S. G. Gorshkov
(C-in-C Naval Forces)

Supreme High Command (VGK)

First Deputy Ministers of Defense

Chief, Main Political Directorate

C-in-Cs of Soviet Forces

General Secretary CPSU

Minister of Defense

Chief of the General Staff

General Staff (Executive Agent of VGK)

Wartime Defense Council

Chairman, KGB

Chairman, USSR Council of Ministers

Chairman, GOSPLAN

Other Party and State Figures as Required

ed by the Communist Party apparatus, which provides for continued Party rule over the Soviet Union during peace or war. The key elements in this command structure are designed to shift to wartime operations with a minimal amount of organizational disruption. The Soviets believe that this command structure provides the national leadership with the flexible and efficient mechanism necessary to meet their peacetime military requirements in domestic and foreign affairs and provides a high degree of confidence that they can control their forces in either conventional or nuclear conflict.

Use of Military Power

Intimidation and Force

Military power is the principal instrument of Soviet expansionist policy. Consequently, the Armed Forces have been readied for war at any level at any time.

The grand strategy of the USSR, however, is to attain its objectives, if possible, by means short of war—capitalizing on the coercive leverage inherent in superior forces, particularly nuclear forces, to instill fear, to erode the West's collective security arrangements and to support subversion. Thus, the primary role of Soviet military power is to provide the essential underpinning for the step by step extension of Soviet influence and control.

Since 1917, the Soviets have, in fact, often used their Armed Forces to pursue foreign policy objectives and extend Soviet boundaries when the risks were low. For example:

• In 1920, the Soviets tried to set up a puppet regime in Poland, but were stopped at Warsaw by Polish forces.

• In 1939, the Red Army partitioned Poland with the Nazis and attacked Finland later that winter.

• In 1940, the Finns were forced to cede considerable territory to the Soviets, and the Red Army occupied Latvia, Lithuania, Estonia and the Romanian province of Bessarabia.

• In 1945-46, the Soviets tried to set up a Soviet regime in northern Iran, which Soviet troops had occupied since 1943.

• The Soviets installed Communist regimes throughout Eastern Europe in 1945-48. The Yugoslav Communist regime, however, with an indigenous political base of broad support and no permanently stationed Red Army forces, broke ties with the USSR in 1948.

• In 1950, the North Korean invasion of South Korea was made possible by Soviet material support. The Soviets moved 20,000 to 25,000 troops to border areas of North Korea, and Soviet pilots defended the Yalu River bridges until the Chinese entered the conflict.

• In 1953, the Soviets assisted the East German regime in putting down a popular uprising.

• In October 1956, Khrushchev threatened to use Soviet military force in Poland, and in October-November 1956, Soviet tanks crushed the Hungarian rebellion.

• In August 1968, Soviet and non-Soviet Warsaw Pact forces occupied Czechoslovakia, in order to destroy a socialist regime "with a human face."

• In 1979, the Soviets invaded Afghanistan and executed one Communist prime minister to install a more tractable one.

• In 1980-81, the threat of Soviet military intervention was used several times to pressure Polish authorities to crack down on the Solidarity Labor Movement, and the Soviets began to mobilize forces for military intervention. Polish imposition of martial law helped to avoid a Soviet invasion.

• More recently, the buildup of SS-20 missiles threatening Europe has been the backdrop for Soviet attempts to turn European public opinion against NATO's program to redress the balance. Similarly, the increase of SS-20 and other Soviet deployments in the Far East has been accompanied by threats and propaganda aimed at impeding any increase in Japanese conventional forces.

While such examples do not argue against either seeking a constructive relationship with the USSR or pressing negotiations for verifiable reductions in arms, they are of importance in providing a clearer understanding of the character of the Soviet regime and the obstacles facing the Free World.

Warfighting Doctrine and Strategy

Soviet military doctrine defines the nature of a future war, probable adversaries, objectives, general characteristics of the forces required and preparedness policies. By Soviet definition, military strategy specifies how the objectives are to be achieved, forces and weapons required, interrelationships among military requirements, economic and technological capabilities, service missions, war management, civil defense, resources and logistics requirements, leadership, command of military forces and an assessment of the strategic views of the probable enemy.

The Soviet military has always recognized the grave consequences of nuclear war. However, changes in the nuclear balance over the past 25 years have led to periodic modifications in Soviet doctrine—in step with major accretions of Soviet nuclear capabilities. In the early 1960s, the Soviet Union envisioned war with the West to be nuclear from the outset; a decade later, doctrine was modified to allow for a conventional phase in a NATO-Warsaw Pact confrontation; and it now appears that the Soviets may theorize that such a major war could remain non-nuclear.

Soviet military doctrine and strategy for global war are:

* A war between the USSR/Warsaw Pact and the US/NATO would be a decisive conflict between "socialism" and "imperialism" to determine which system would prevail.
* The war would be a "just" war for the USSR but "unjust" for the West.
* If war occurs, the USSR and its Allies would seek to defeat enemy military forces globally and occupy enemy territory in Eurasia. The war might begin under a variety of circumstances; it might be relatively brief—a few weeks; it could turn into a more protracted conflict.
* The Soviets perceive that any conflict between themselves and the West could easily escalate to the nuclear level. They also believe that an effective nuclear strategy and execution would decide the course of such conflict. Nonetheless, they believe that territory can be held only with troops and that even on a nuclear battlefield final victory could only be won by ground armies reaching and controlling their ultimate objectives. Hence, Soviet doctrine calls for continuing conventional arms offen-

sives during and after any nuclear phase of a general war.
* Priority targets of all Soviet forces would be the enemy's nuclear delivery systems and weapons, nuclear command, control and communications, air defenses and politico-administrative centers.

Specific Soviet aims in war would be:
* to ensure continuity of Communist Party control over the Soviet Government, military, police and internal security organs and the population,
* to minimize losses to Soviet leadership, scientific-technical elites and other essential personnel, to the general population and to the economy; to repair immediate damage, and to organize recovery,
* to provide continuity of the Soviet politico-military-economic system;
* to defeat NATO forces, occupy, NATO countries and use Europe's economic assets to assist Soviet recovery,
* to neutralize the United States and China by disorganizing and destroying their military forces, and
* to dominate the post-war world in which "socialism" will have replaced "imperialism" as the basic politico-economic system in all nations.

Decisionmaking Process

The attainment of military goals and objectives, the use of force or threat of use of force to suppress domestic dissent and the application or threat of use of force in foreign policy are facilitated by the governmental structure in the Soviet Union. Soviet leaders today perpetuate a powerful and rigidly centralized state that strives to control every national resource, under the guise of ensuring national survival in a hostile environment. This they achieve through the one-party system in which the Communist Party apparatus has an undisputed monopoly of power over the decisionmaking process. This monopoly was formally recognized in the 1977 Constitution, which described the Party as the leading and guiding force of Soviet society and the nucleus of its political system for all State and public organizations.

Official Party representatives permeate and control the State and military apparatus. Military doctrine, national security policies, eco-

SOVIE (SOVIET...)

BALTIC FLEET

PRINCIPAL SURFACE COMBATANTS	42
OTHER COMBATANT SHIPS	99
SUBMARINES	32
NAVAL AVIATION	275

NORTHERN FLEET

AIRCRAFT CARRIERS
PRINCIPAL SURFACE COMBATANTS
OTHER COMBATANT SHIPS
SUBMARINES
NAVAL AVIATION

55 NON-SOVIET WARSAW
PACT DIVISIONS

30 SOVIET
DIVISIONS

EASTERN EUROPE

Murmansk

Leningrad

Moscow

82 DIVISIONS

Sevastopol

USSR

BLACK SEA FLEET/
CASPIAN FLOTILLA

AIRCRAFT CARRIERS	1
PRINCIPAL SURFACE COMBATANTS	76
OTHER COMBATANT SHIPS	85
SUBMARINES	24
NAVAL AVIATION	405

30 DIVISIONS

NUCLEAR FORCES

ICBMs		LRINF		SLBMs		BOMBERS		TACTICAL AIRCRAFT	
SS-11	520	SS-4	224	SS-N-5	45	BACKFIRE	235*		
SS-13	60	SS-20	378	SS-N-6	368	BISON	45		
SS-17	150			SS-N-8	292	BEAR	115+		
SS-18	308			SS-N-17	12	BADGER	316	TACTICAL	
SS-19	360			SS-N-18	224	BLINDER	139	AIRCRAFT	6,280
				SS-N-20	40				

* Including 105 in
Soviet Naval Aviation.

ILITARY FORCES

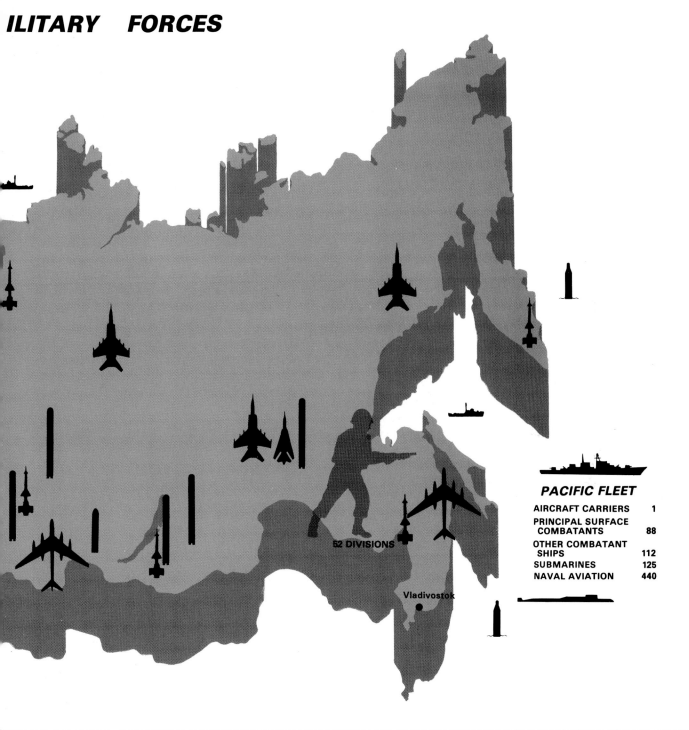

52 DIVISIONS

Vladivostok

PACIFIC FLEET

AIRCRAFT CARRIERS	1
PRINCIPAL SURFACE COMBATANTS	88
OTHER COMBATANT SHIPS	112
SUBMARINES	125
NAVAL AVIATION	440

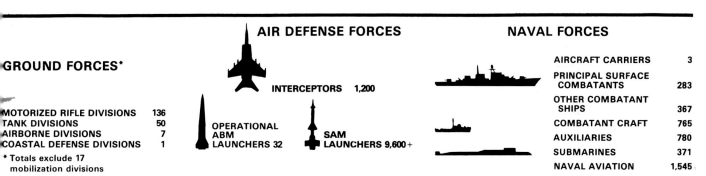

GROUND FORCES*

MOTORIZED RIFLE DIVISIONS	136
TANK DIVISIONS	50
AIRBORNE DIVISIONS	7
COASTAL DEFENSE DIVISIONS	1

* Totals exclude 17 mobilization divisions

AIR DEFENSE FORCES

INTERCEPTORS 1,200

OPERATIONAL ABM LAUNCHERS 32

SAM LAUNCHERS 9,600+

NAVAL FORCES

AIRCRAFT CARRIERS	3
PRINCIPAL SURFACE COMBATANTS	283
OTHER COMBATANT SHIPS	367
COMBATANT CRAFT	765
AUXILIARIES	780
SUBMARINES	371
NAVAL AVIATION	1,545

nomic planning and administration are all developed and coordinated by the Party hierarchy. This concentration of power in the hands of a political elite is most evident at the national level, where Party, State and military responsibilities are often within the purview of one individual.

The job of the Soviet Government is to implement Party policy under the eye of the ever-present Party officials. The Party pervades all Soviet organizations, official and unofficial. All are penetrated and monitored by the Party watchdog, the Committee for State Security (KGB). Several members of the Politburo simultaneously hold key posts in the state apparatus. Almost without exception, government ministers and senior military commanders are members of the CPSU Central Committee. All responsible government positions are filled by trusted Party members.

Centers of political power outside the Party are prohibited in the USSR; thus, Soviet decisionmaking can produce policies with a force and constancy not achievable in democratic and pluralistic political systems. The relatively small number of senior Party members holding key Party and government positions, their age and often long tenure have produced a well-entrenched, rather homogeneous decisionmaking elite. This Party elite has a shared heritage and maintains common interests as to basic directions in domestic and foreign policy, a factor which helps to account for the marked continuity of its policies.

The late General Secretary Andropov served as an excellent example of this leadership elite and of the total domination of the Communist Party over all aspects of Soviet affairs. His accumulated experience as a Party member extended over four decades. He worked both at the regional and national level in the Party apparatus. As Ambassador to Hungary, Andropov acquired a knowledge of the Soviet style of diplomacy and played a key role in the Soviet invasion in 1956. From 1967 to 1982, he headed the KGB and, in that capacity, engineered the crackdown on the Soviet human rights/dissident movement. Most recently, and until his death, Andropov held three of the most important positions in the Soviet Union: General Secretary of the Communist Party, Head of State and Supreme Commander in Chief of the Armed Forces.

The power wielded by the General Secretary is derived from the Party itself. At the apex of the Party's centralized, hierarchical structure is the Politburo, which exercises power through a disciplined Party bureaucracy. Essential support to the Politburo's national decisionmaking role is provided by the Central Committee (CC) Secretariat. At present, it consists of 10 members, headed by a General Secretary, and is concerned with the full spectrum of national policy issues, as well as monitoring government performance and controlling lower-level Party appointments, ideology and internal Party matters. The CC Secretariat is supported by a staff of several thousand full-time employees. This staff is organized into over 20 departments paralleling elements of the government. Through these mechanisms, the Party maintains control of the day-to-day activities of the Soviet State.

The Military in Soviet Society

In Soviet society, military forces exist not as a separate institution, but rather as an inherent part of the Soviet system. One is just

Motorized infantry troops on tactical exercise: the Soviet Law on Universal Military Service specifies that every male citizen is subject to military service until age 50.

as likely to find a uniformed soldier in the offices of a research institute as in the barracks of a field unit.

The Soviet Union maintains Armed Forces both for external and for internal operations. These include five combat services: Strategic Rocket, Air, Ground, Naval and Air Defense Forces. Additionally, they include the troops of the Committee for State Security (KGB) and the Ministry of Internal Affairs (MVD).

KGB troops consist of at least 200,000-to-250,000 Border Guards and another 30,000-to-50,000 troops assigned to special communica-

Some 250,000 KGB troops are used primarily for internal operations, to seal Soviet borders.

ing the border clashes with the Chinese in 1967-69. The principal purpose of the KGB's Border Troops, however, is to seal Soviet borders.

The MVD currently has about 30 divisions. MVD troops reinforce police, when necessary, to quell internal disturbances. In addition, MVD troops man the watch towers of the Soviet Union's concentration camps (GULAG) and guard the inmates working on forced labor projects.

The Soviet obsession with security has played a central role in influencing the Party's approach to the development of the Soviet State and the evolution of its Armed Forces. From the time the Communists first seized power, they have cultivated a special relationship with the Armed Forces. M.V. Frunze, the Bolshevik military leader who replaced Leon Trotsky in 1925 as head of the Red Army, argued that the next war could be won only through the "militarization of the entire population."

The Great Patriotic War, as the Soviets call

tions units charged with providing reliable and secure communications to top Party and government entities.

KGB Border Troops have heavy equipment, including tanks and artillery, and sometimes engage external forces. This was the case dur-

KGB Border Guard Force Concentration

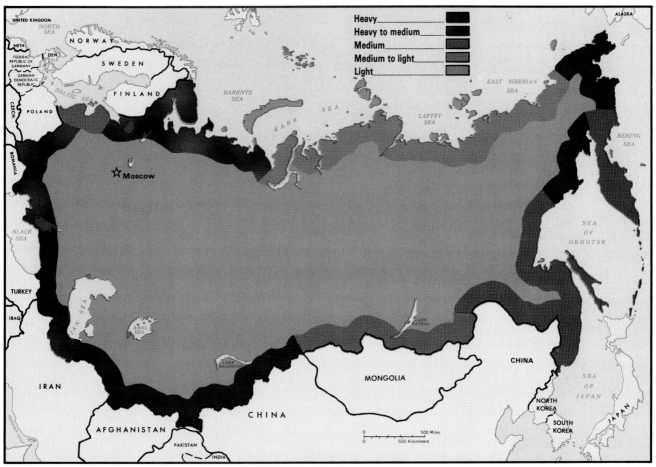

Chapter I The Soviet Military Establishment

For two decades, the USSR has pressed ahead with a large naval construction program, with the continuing introduction of new classes of surface warships, submarines and aircraft carriers, including the MINSK of the KIEV-Class carriers.

World War II, bore out Frunze's predictions. The Soviets mobilized the entire country behind the war effort. That undertaking left a mark on Soviet society that is evident to this day. The Party and the government use this to remind Soviet citizens of the sacrifices made and to emphasize the importance of military preparedness. The war is still glorified and commemorated. Anniversaries of key battles are honored. In addition, the Armed Forces always play a prominent role in important holidays, such as the annual November celebrations of the Bolshevik Revolution.

The constant reminders of the Great Patriotic War are part of a broader military presence that every Soviet citizen is subjected to in a strict, formalized manner. The Soviet Law on Universal Military Service specifies that every male citizen is subject to military service until age 50 and that military service in the ranks of the Armed Forces of the USSR is an honorable duty of Soviet citizens. The Soviet system of universal military service is supported by a vast military-educational complex designed to prepare the individual for the Armed Forces long before he or she enters the service.

Premilitary training occurs both in the school system and through a number of official youth organizations. Soviet students are taught to respect the importance of military service and to honor the role of the Armed Forces in society. Grade school children learn of the military through visits to war memorials, class projects that eulogize war heroes and glorify the campaigns of local military units, and through direct contact with forces stationed in the area. Soviet boys and girls, in the 8-to-15 age group, generally join the Pioneers, an organization supported by the CPSU. The Pioneers sponsor numerous activities, including nationwide military-sports games such as the Zarnitsa. Youth battalions, organized as military units, compete in the annual Zarnitsa for much coveted citations. The Pioneers have other responsibilities, such as guarding war monuments and shrines.

In addition to the Pioneers, a Soviet 14-year-old is also likely to join a unit of the Volunteer Society for Cooperation with the Army, Aviation and the Fleet, known by its acronym DOSAAF. DOSAAF is an organization of over 330,000 different units scattered throughout the USSR, numbering over 80 million students and workers.

DOSAAF units play an important role in providing pre-service basic training to Soviet youth. Special courses give students the opportunity to operate military equipment. Through various sports functions, young people can learn other skills that prepare them for military service, including sharpshooting, parachuting and scuba diving. DOSAAF's role, as part of the Soviet military-educational system is perhaps best symbolized by the fact that its chief is a Soviet Navy Fleet Admiral, Georgiy M. Yegorov.

Military education in the Soviet Union does not focus on the youth alone. Citizens can be called back into active service until age 50. In addition, large numbers of military academies and schools provide specialist training for both active duty and reserve officers. Finally, the public at large participates in a nationwide civil defense educational program that is the responsibility of the Ministry of Defense and run by an active-duty general officer.

Soviet Military Power

In his speech accepting the post of General Secretary of the Soviet Communist Party, the late Yuri Andropov stated that, "We well know that peace cannot be begged from the imperialists. It can only be defended by relying on the invincible might of the Soviet Armed Forces."

This Soviet commitment to its Armed Forces was reaffirmed by General Secretary Chernenko on his accession to the top leadership role when he declared, "We will further see to it that our country's defense capability is strengthened, that we have enough means to cool the hotheads of militant adventurists. This, comrades, is a very substantial prerequisite for preserving peace."

The USSR's willingness to threaten and use military force under certain conditions to achieve the objectives of the State and the prominent role of the military in Soviet society present a serious challenge to world peace. The role and structure of the military establishment, however threatening, do not portray the full picture. The State is fully committed to developing, supporting and sustaining military forces for use internally, regionally and globally. The dedication of the Soviet leadership and Armed Forces to these objectives is examined in the following chapters.

Chapter II

Forces for Global Warfare

Soviet leaders, since Khrushchev's time, have followed a consistent policy for the development of their intercontinental forces. Their main objective has been to capitalize, in peacetime, on the coercive leverage inherent in powerful nuclear forces to induce paralysis in weapons programs and create political disarray in the free societies. In wartime, they would regard the threat or actual use of those forces as the key to the successful prosecution of the conflict.

In a global conflict, Soviet strategic policy would seek the destruction of Western nuclear forces on the ground and in flight to their targets, the capability to ensure national survival should nuclear weapons reach the Soviet homeland and the ability to support and sustain combined arms combat in several theaters of military operations. From these policy directives come several overarching strategic wartime missions:

- protect the Soviet State,
- support the land war in Eurasia and
- eliminate the US capability to conduct or support warfare at home and beyond its own shores.

Protection of the Soviet State, the most difficult mission, would involve:

- disruption and destruction of the West's nuclear-associated command, control and communications,
- destruction or neutralization of as many of the West's nuclear weapons as possible on the ground or at sea before they could be launched,

The submarine-launched, nuclear-armed SS-NX-21 cruise missile is one of three new long-range land-attack cruise missile systems nearing deployment, which — with their high accuracy and 3,000-kilo-meter range — will add still another dimension to the strategic offensive threat posed by the Armed Forces of the Soviet Union.

• interception and destruction of surviving weapons—aircraft and missiles—before they reach targets and

• protection of the Party, the State and industrial infrastructure and the essential working population against those weapons that reach their targets.

Theater and strategic forces and programs in place or under active development designed to accomplish these tasks include:

• hard-target-capable Intercontinental Ballistic Missiles (ICBMs), Longer-Range Intermediate-Range Nuclear Force (LRINF) missiles and land-based cruise missiles,

• bombers and air-launched cruise missiles (ALCMs) capable of penetrating US defensive systems,

• Submarine Launched Ballistic Missiles (SLBMs) and cruise missiles on various platforms,

• antisubmarine warfare (ASW) forces capable of attacking US nuclear-powered ballistic missile submarines (SSBNs),

• air and missile defenses, including early warning satellites and radars, interceptor aircraft, surface-to-air missiles (SAMs), antiballistic missile (ABM) radars and interceptors and some anti-aircraft artillery,

• antisatellite weapons,

• passive defense forces, including civil defense forces, and countermeasures troops and equipment devoted to confusing incoming aircraft and

• hardened facilities numbering in the thousands, command vehicles and evacuation plans designed to protect Party, military, governmental and industrial staffs, essential workers and, to the extent possible, the general population.

Supporting a land war in Eurasia and eliminating the US capacity to fight and support conflict would require the capability to employ theater and strategic forces over a variety of ranges and the destruction of:

• other military-associated command and control,

• war-supporting industries, arsenals and major military facilities,

• ports and airfields in the United States and those along sea and air routes to European and Asian theaters of war and

• satellite surveillance sensors,

ground-based surveillance sensors, facilities and communications.

Offensive forces (ICBMs, LRINF, SLBMs, cruise missiles and bombers) and antisatellite weapons would generally be assigned these tasks. In some cases, special purpose forces could be used for these missions, especially in Eurasia. These tasks would be generally less demanding than those in the prime category.

Soviet nuclear forces are designed to fulfill their missions under the best and worst of circumstances. In the context of a nuclear war, the Soviets believe the most favorable circumstance would be a preemptive strike; the least favorable would be a follow-on strike after nuclear weapons hit the USSR. Between would be launch-under-attack; that is, executing offensive operations after weapons aimed at the USSR had been launched. The Soviets have wide-ranging programs intended to enable nuclear forces to operate under each of these circumstances. Moreover, the Soviets appear to believe that nuclear war might last for weeks or even months and have factored this into their force development.

• In a preemptive strike, the essentials would be effective coordination of the strike and sound intelligence on Western intentions. Soviet nuclear forces routinely practice command and control under various conditions. During wartime, the main mission of Soviet intelligence would be to determine the West's courses of action.

• Launch-under-attack circumstances would place the greatest stress on attack warning systems and launch coordination. To meet this demand, the Soviets have established a satellite-based ICBM launch detection system, built an over-the-horizon radar missile launch detection system to back up the satellites and have large phased-array radars ringing the USSR. These warning devices could give the Soviet leadership time to launch their forces after an enemy strike had been launched. To prepare for this possibility, the Soviets practice launching weapons under stringent time constraints.

• Follow-on strikes would stress the survivability of the command, control and communications systems as well as the weapons themselves. The Soviets have invested heavily in providing this

Selected Nuclear Forces

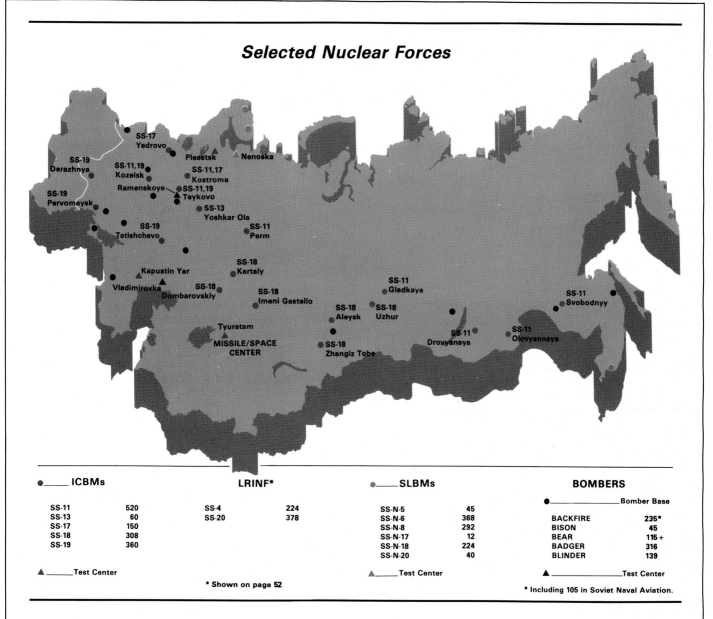

ICBMs		LRINF*		SLBMs		BOMBERS	
● ICBMs				● SLBMs		● Bomber Base	
SS-11	520	SS-4	224	SS-N-5	45		
SS-13	60	SS-20	378	SS-N-6	368	BACKFIRE	235*
SS-17	150			SS-N-8	292	BISON	45
SS-18	308			SS-N-17	12	BEAR	115 +
SS-19	360			SS-N-18	224	BADGER	316
				SS-N-20	40	BLINDER	139
▲ Test Center				▲ Test Center		▲ Test Center	
		* Shown on page 52				* Including 105 in Soviet Naval Aviation.	

survivability. The SS-17, SS-18 and SS-19 ICBMs are housed in the world's hardest silos. Silo deployment has been adopted for ABMs as well. To increase survivability, the SS-20 LRINF missile is mobile. Mobile ICBMs are under development, and a mobile strategic surface-to-air missile is being tested. The launch control facilities for offensive missiles are housed in very hard silos or on off-road vehicles. Communications are redundant and hardened. Higher commands have multiple vehicles and aircraft available for their use as alternate command posts. Bombers have alert procedures and dispersal airfields. Ballistic missile submarines could be placed in tunnels near their home ports, submerged in deep fjords just off their piers, dispersed or protected by Soviet surface and submarine forces.

• The belief that war might be protracted has led to the USSR's emphasis on survivability along with war reserves, protection for people and equipment and the capacity to reload launchers. For their ICBM, LRINF and air defense forces, the Soviets have stocked extra missiles, propellants and warheads throughout the USSR. Some ICBM silo launchers could be reloaded, and provision has been made for the decontamination of those launchers. Plans for the survival of necessary

At left, a Soviet missile crew loads an SS-9 ICBM into a silo in the late 1960s. Starting in 1970, SS-9 silos were rebuilt to increase their survivability and accommodate the SS-18 heavy ICBM. Unlike the SS-9, the SS-18 is transported and loaded into its silo in a canister. Special silo-loading equipment, above, is used with the SS-18 ICBM.

equipment and personnel have been developed and practiced. In addition, resupply systems are available to reload Soviet SSBNs in protected waters.

Even with these ambitious development and deployment programs over the years, the Soviets are continuing to modernize all aspects of their strategic forces. The Soviet leadership has also been directing a campaign to support and amplify ongoing anti-nuclear movements in the West, in order to influence, delay or frustrate Western nuclear program development. Using this two-pronged approach, Moscow seeks new gains in relative capability despite the drive of Western governments to redress the imbalance that has developed over the past decade.

Because of the open nature of US society, and the fact that much US technology is unclassified, the Soviets have been able to take advantage of US research and development to accelerate their already considerable technological effort. Information and hardware already obtained have saved the USSR billions of dollars and resulted in the achievement of some military capabilities years in advance of what could have been achieved if they were solely dependent on their own resources.

Intercontinental Attack

Intercontinental Ballistic Missiles

Current Systems and Force Levels. The operational Soviet ICBM force is made up of 1,398 silo launchers. Some 818 of these launchers have been rebuilt since 1972. Nearly half of these silos are new versions of the original designs and have been reconstructed or modified in the past 5 years. All of these 818 silos have been hardened, better to withstand attack by currently operational US ICBMs, and house the world's most modern deployed ICBMs—the SS-17 Mod 3 (150 silos), the SS-18 Mod 4 (308) and the SS-19 Mod 3 (360). Deployment of these ICBMs began only 5 years ago.

The SS-18 and SS-19 ICBMs are at least as accurate and possibly more accurate and carry more Multiple Independently Targetable Reentry Vehicles (MIRVs) than the MINUTEMAN III, the most modern operational US ICBM. The SS-18 Mod 4 carries 10 MIRVs, and the SS-19 Mod 3 carries six whereas the MINUTEMAN III carries only three. The SS-18 Mod 4 was specifically designed to attack and destroy ICBM silos and other hardened targets in the United States. Each of its 10 warheads has more than 20 times the destructive power of the nuclear devices developed during World War II. The force of SS-18 Mod 4s currently deployed has the capability to destroy more than 80 percent of the US ICBM silo launchers using two nuclear warheads against each US silo. The SS-19 Mod 3 has nearly identical capabilities. In addition, the SS-19 Mod 3 could be used against targets in Eurasia. The SS-17 Mod 3 is a somewhat less-capable ICBM than the SS-19, but it has similar targeting flexibility.

The remaining 580 Soviet ICBM silos are fitted with the SS-11—420 SS-11 Mod 2/3s and 100 SS-11 Mod 1s—and 60 SS-13 Mod 2s. These ICBMs are of older vintage, 1966 and 1973 initial deployments respectively, are housed in less-survivable silos and are considerably less capable. Nevertheless, their destructive potential against softer area targets in the United States and Eurasia is significant in terms of many of the Soviet nuclear tasks outlined above.

The SS-16 is a three-stage, solid-propellant, single-RV ICBM that the Soviets claim has not been deployed. The system was first tested in 1972; the last known test took place in 1976. The SS-20 LRINF missile is closely related to the SS-16. The SS-16 probably was intended originally for both silo and mobile deployment, using equipment and a basing arrangement comparable to that used with the

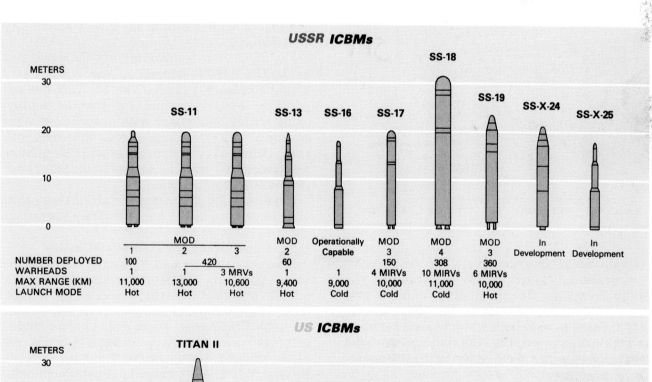

	MOD			MOD	Operationally	MOD	MOD	MOD	In	In
	1	2	3	2	Capable	3	4	3	Development	Development
NUMBER DEPLOYED	100		420	60		150	308	360		
WARHEADS	1	1	3 MRVs	1	1	4 MIRVs	10 MIRVs	6 MIRVs		
MAX RANGE (KM)	11,000	13,000	10,600	9,400	9,000	10,000	11,000	10,000		
LAUNCH MODE	Hot	Hot	Hot	Hot	Cold	Cold	Cold	Hot		

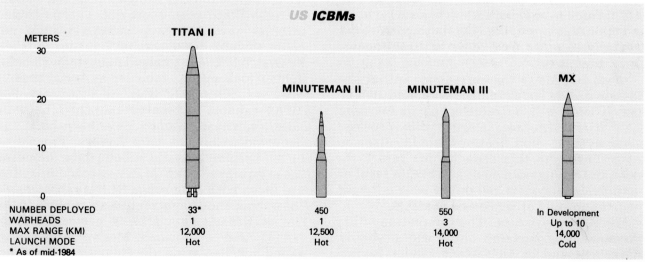

	TITAN II	MINUTEMAN II	MINUTEMAN III	MX
NUMBER DEPLOYED	33*	450	550	In Development
WARHEADS	1	1	3	Up to 10
MAX RANGE (KM)	12,000	12,500	14,000	14,000
LAUNCH MODE	Hot	Hot	Hot	Cold

* As of mid-1984

SS-20. The Soviet Union agreed in SALT II not to produce, test, or deploy ICBMs of the SS-16 type and, in particular, not to produce the SS-16 third stage, the RV or the appropriate device for targeting the RV of that missile. Available information does not allow a conclusive judgment on whether the Soviets deployed the SS-16, but does indicate probable deployment.

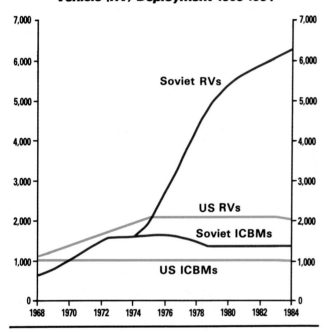

US and Soviet ICBM Launcher and Reentry Vehicle (RV) Deployment 1968-1984

Deployment programs for all of the currently operational Soviet ICBM systems are virtually complete. The command, control and communications structure for the Soviet ICBM force is modern and highly survivable, and the reliability of the ICBMs themselves is regularly sampled by live firings from operational complexes.

Those ICBMs in the current force that the Soviets decide not to replace with modified or new ICBMs will be refurbished to increase their useful lifetime. During this process, some system modifications could also be made. Owing to this capacity for refurbishment, the Soviets can sustain a higher level of confidence in system reliability over a longer term than would otherwise be possible.

Force Developments. The completion of deployment programs now under way probably marks the end of significant Soviet invest-

ment in silo-launchers and in the development of wholly new liquid-propellant ICBMs. At least one additional modified version of both the SS-18 and SS-19, however, is likely to be produced and deployed in existing silos in the future.

Despite these development programs, the Soviets appear to be planning on new, solid-propellant ICBMs to redress future mission shortfalls in counterforce capability and survivability. Two new solid-propellant ICBMs, the medium-sized SS-X-24 and the smaller SS-X-25, are being tested from the range head at Plesetsk in the Soviet north. Available evidence suggests mobile as well as silo deployment for both systems.

The SS-X-24 will probably be silo-deployed at first. Mobile deployment could follow several years after initial operational capability is achieved in 1985. This ICBM is likely to be even more accurate than the SS-18 Mod 4 and SS-19 Mod 3.

The SS-X-25 is approximately the same size as the US MINUTEMAN ICBM. It will carry a single reentry vehicle. The SS-X-25 has apparently been designed for mobile deployment, with a home base with launcher garages equipped with sliding roofs; massive, off-road, wheeled transporter-erector-launchers; and necessary mobile support equipment for refires from the launcher.

Development programs for all of these missiles have been under way for many years.

Submarine-Launched Ballistic Missiles
Current Systems and Force Levels. The Soviets maintain the world's largest ballistic missile submarine force for strategic attack. As of March 1984, the force numbered 64 submarines fitted with some 936 nuclear-tipped missiles. Two of these submarines do not count toward the 62 SSBN limit established by SALT I. These totals also exclude 15 older submarines with 45 missiles assigned theater missions. Sixteen SSBNs are fitted with 264 MIRV-capable submarine-launched ballistic missiles. These 16 units have been built and deployed within the past 7 years. Two-thirds of the ballistic missile submarines, including those equipped with MIRV-capable missiles, are fitted with long-range SLBMs that enable the submarines to patrol in waters close to the Soviet Union. This affords protection from NATO ASW operations. Moreover, the long-range missiles allow the Soviets to fire from

Since the early 1960s, the Soviets have been perfecting mobile missile deployment techniques. Shown at top is the SS-X-15 mobile shorter-range ICBM. At left is the mobile SS-X-14 LRINF missile being erected for launch. Both systems were in test in the late 1960s; neither was deployed. The development of the SS-16, SS-20 and SS-X-25 mobile missiles was founded on the technologies these systems represented.

home ports, if necessary, and still strike targets in the United States.

Two units of the most modern Soviet ballistic missile submarine, the TYPHOON, have already been built. One is operational and the other soon will be. Each carries 20 SS-N-20 solid-propellant, MIRVed SLBMs. The TYPHOON is the world's largest submarine, with a displacement of 25,000 tons, one-third greater than the US TRIDENT. The submarine can operate under the Arctic Ocean ice cap, adding further to the protection afforded by the 8,300-kilometer range of the SS-N-20 SLBM. Three to four additional TYPHOONs are probably now under construction, and, by the early 1990s, the Soviets could have as many as eight of these potent weapons systems in their operational force.

In accord with the SALT I Interim Agreement, the Soviets have, since 1978, removed 10 YANKEE I units from service as ballistic missile submarines. These units had to be removed as newer submarines were produced in order for the overall Soviet SSBN force to stay within the 62 modern SSBN/950 SLBM limits established in 1972. These YANKEEs, however, have not been scrapped and some may be returned to service as attack or cruise missile submarines.

In a further development with the YANKEE SSBN force, the Soviets may have begun to assign theater attack missions to some of the 23 remaining YANKEE I submarines. However, YANKEE patrols targeted against the United States continue.

Force Developments. The Soviets have begun flight-tests of a new, large, liquid-propelled, long-range SLBM—the SS-NX-23. This system is likely to be deployed as a replacement for the SS-N-18 SLBM carried by the DELTA III SSBN. The SS-NX-23 will have greater throwweight, carry more warheads and be more accurate than the SS-N-18.

Based on past Soviet practice, before the end of the 1980s, they may initiate testing of

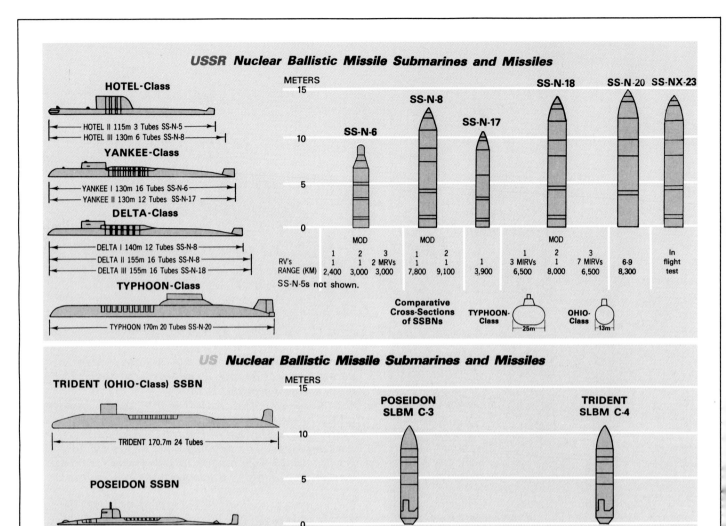

USSR Nuclear Ballistic Missile Submarines and Missiles

HOTEL-Class
- HOTEL II 115m 3 Tubes SS-N-5
- HOTEL III 130m 6 Tubes SS-N-8

YANKEE-Class
- YANKEE I 130m 16 Tubes SS-N-6
- YANKEE II 130m 12 Tubes SS-N-17

DELTA-Class
- DELTA I 140m 12 Tubes SS-N-8
- DELTA II 155m 16 Tubes SS-N-8
- DELTA III 155m 16 Tubes SS-N-18

TYPHOON-Class
- TYPHOON 170m 20 Tubes SS-N-20

METERS 15

SS-N-6, SS-N-8, SS-N-17, SS-N-18, SS-N-20, SS-NX-23

	SS-N-6 MOD			SS-N-8 MOD		SS-N-17	SS-N-18 MOD			SS-N-20	SS-NX-23
RV's	1	2	3 2 MRVs	1	2	1	1 3 MIRVs	2	3 7 MIRVs	6-9	In flight test
RANGE (KM)	2,400	3,000	3,000	7,800	9,100	3,900	6,500	8,000	6,500	8,300	

SS-N-5s not shown.

Comparative Cross-Sections of SSBNs: TYPHOON-Class 25m, OHIO-Class 13m

US Nuclear Ballistic Missile Submarines and Missiles

TRIDENT (OHIO-Class) SSBN
- TRIDENT 170.7m 24 Tubes

POSEIDON SSBN
- POSEIDON 129.5m 16 Tubes

METERS 15

	POSEIDON SLBM C-3	TRIDENT SLBM C-4
RV's	10	8
RANGE (KM)	4,000	7,400

Modern SSBN Force Levels

US
3 OHIO

US
31 LAFAYETTE/
BEN. FRANKLIN
1 OHIO

USSR
21 DELTA
15 YANKEE
2 TYPHOON

USSR
15 DELTA
9 YANKEE

US and Soviet SLBM Launcher and Reentry Vehicle (RV) Deployment 1968-1984

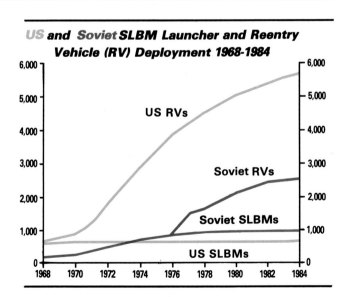

modified versions of the SS-NX-23 and the SS-N-20. Both of these systems are likely to be more accurate than their predecessors.

The Soviets emphasize redundant and timely command and control for their military forces, especially those for intercontinental attack. The Soviets may deploy an extremely low frequency (ELF) communications system that will enable them to contact the SSBNs under most operating conditions.

DELTA III SSBN, equipped with 16 MIRVed SS-N-18 SLBMs.

Strategic Aviation

Current Systems and Force Levels. Soviet strategic bombers and strike aircraft are controlled by the central Soviet leadership using five air armies as intermediate commands. These armies were established to place Soviet strategic aircraft on a footing in peacetime that would facilitate the transition to wartime. These armies are focused on potential conflict in Europe, Asia and the United States.

Strategic aviation assets include some 170 BEAR and BISON bombers, 235 BACKFIRE bombers (including 105 BACKFIRE bombers in Soviet Naval Aviation). The Soviets also

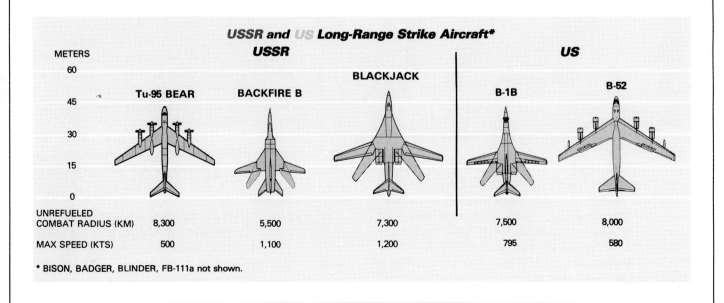

USSR and US Long-Range Strike Aircraft*

METERS	USSR			US	
	Tu-95 BEAR	BACKFIRE B	BLACKJACK	B-1B	B-52
UNREFUELED COMBAT RADIUS (KM)	8,300	5,500	7,300	7,500	8,000
MAX SPEED (KTS)	500	1,100	1,200	795	580

* BISON, BADGER, BLINDER, FB-111a not shown.

Chapter II Forces for Global Warfare

have 455 medium-range BLINDER and BADGER bombers, 450 shorter-range FENC-ER strike aircraft and 530 tanker, reconnaissance and electronic warfare aircraft. The Soviets have allocated these aircraft among the five air armies to provide support for specific theaters of military operations but also to assure the flexibility to reallocate aircraft as necessary during wartime. The intercontinental BEAR and BISON bombers are available for maritime and Eurasian missions, and the BACKFIRE is clearly capable of use against the United States. This flexibility allows the Soviets to focus their strategic air assets as circumstances dictate.

The Soviets have taken recent steps that indicate greatly increased interest in the long-

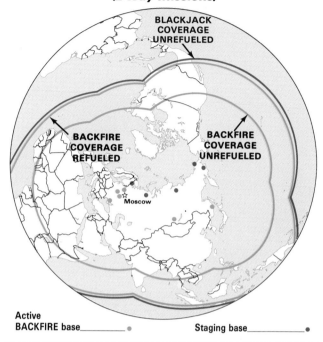

BLACKJACK and BACKFIRE Coverage from Soviet Bases (2-Way Missions)

US and SOVIET Intercontinental-Capable Bombers[1]

Inventory

(line graph: vertical axis 0 to 500 in increments of 50, horizontal axis Years 1979 to 1984. Lines labeled "US", "USSR", and "USSR (excluding aircraft assigned to Naval Aviation)")

Year

[1] US data include B-52, FB-111a ; Soviet data include BEAR, BISON and BACKFIRE.

range strategic bomber. An entirely new variant of the BEAR bomber (BEAR H), probably designed to carry long-range cruise missiles, is now in production—the first new production of a strike version of the BEAR airframe in over 15 years. In addition, older BEAR air-to-surface missile (ASM) carrying aircraft are being reconfigured to carry the newer, super-

sonic AS-4 ASM in place of subsonic AS-3s. Several of these reconfigurations (BEAR G) have been completed. With the new BEAR H in series production, the decline in the inventory of BEAR and BISON aircraft characteristic of recent years has been reversed. The Soviets today have more bombers operational than just a few years ago.

The BACKFIRE is the most modern operational Soviet bomber. The Soviets continue to produce the aircraft at a rate of about 30 per year; this production rate is likely to be maintained at least through the end of the decade. The original design has been modified several times and further modifications are likely to be made to upgrade aircraft performance. The BACKFIRE is a long-range aircraft capable of performing nuclear strike, conventional attack, anti-ship and reconnaissance missions. Its low-level penetration features make it a more survivable system than its predecessors. The BACKFIRE has sufficient range/radius capabilities for it to be employed effectively against the contiguous United States on high-altitude subsonic missions. Its low-altitude supersonic dash capabilities make it a formidable weapon in support of military operations in Europe and Asia as well. The

The Tupolev *BACKFIRE* supersonic bomber is designed to carry the *AS-4 KITCHEN* air-to-surface missile mounted partially in its fuselage, left and at top. The *BACKFIRE* can also carry two wing-mounted AS-4s on the pylons visible in the photograph at top.

BACKFIRE can be equipped with a probe to permit inflight refueling; this would further increase its range and radius capabilities.

The Soviets have some FENCER strike aircraft assigned to strategic aviation. The FENCER is a supersonic, variable-geometry, all-weather fighter-bomber that first reached operational status in 1974. Three variants have been developed, the most recent introduced in 1981. The aircraft is still in production, and the number assigned to strategic aviation is likely to increase by 50 percent over the next few years.

Force Developments. The new Soviet long-range bomber—the BLACKJACK—is still in the flight-test stage of development. The

BLACKJACK is larger than the US B-1B, probably will be somewhat faster and may have about the same combat radius. This new bomber could reach operational status in 1987. The BLACKJACK will be capable of carrying cruise missiles, bombs or a combination of both. It probably will first replace the much less capable BISON bomber and then the BEAR A bomber.

A new aerial-refueling tanker aircraft, based on the Il-76/ CANDID, has been under development for several years. When deployed in the near future, the new tanker will support tactical and strategic aircraft and significantly improve the ability of Soviet aircraft to conduct longer-range operations.

The VICTOR III attack submarine could carry the SS-NX-21 cruise missile.

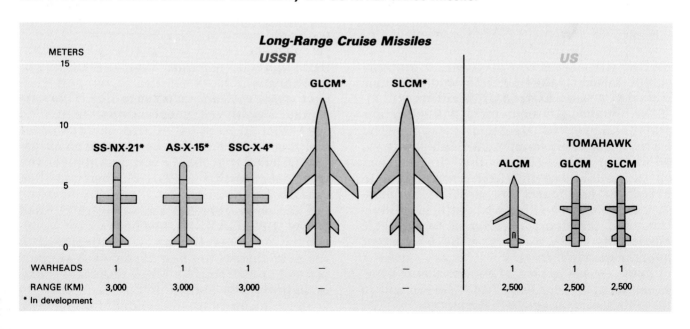

WARHEADS	1	1	1	—	—		1	1	1
RANGE (KM)	3,000	3,000	3,000	—	—		2,500	2,500	2,500

* In development

Long-Range Cruise Missiles

Force Developments. The Soviets are developing five new, long-range cruise missile systems. Three of these are variants of a small subsonic, low-altitude cruise missile similar in design to the US TOMAHAWK. These variants have a range of about 3,000 kilometers. The two others are variants of a larger system probably designed for long-range operations. This system has no US counterpart.

The three smaller cruise missiles are being developed for launch from sea-, ground- and air-based platforms respectively. The sea-based variant, the SS-NX-21, is small enough to be fired from standard Soviet torpedo tubes. Candidate launch platforms for the SS-NX-21 include: the existing VICTOR III SSN, a new YANKEE-Class SSN, the new MIKE-Class SSN (possibly a follow-on to the ALFA-Class high-speed, deep-diving SSN) and the new SIERRA-Class SSN (possibly a follow-on to the VICTOR III). The SS-NX-21 probably will become operational this year. SS-NX-21s carried by submarines could be deployed near US coasts.

The ground-based SSC-X-4 variant of the small cruise missile may not be ready for operational deployment until about 1985. Its range and the likelihood that the Soviets will not deploy the system outside the USSR indicate that its mission will be in support of theater operations. The system will be mobile and probably follow operational procedures like those of the SS-20 LRINF missile.

The air-launched version of this cruise missile—the AS-X-15—could reach initial operational status this year on the new BEAR H ALCM carrier aircraft. The system could also be deployed on BLACKJACK bombers when that aircraft reaches operational status. The combination of the AS-X-15 and the new BEAR H and BLACKJACK bombers will increase Soviet strategic intercontinental air power in the late 1980s.

The larger cruise missile, which has not yet been designated, will have sea- and ground-based variants. Both the sea- and ground-based versions could be operational within the next 2 years.

When first deployed, each of these five cruise missiles will be fitted with nuclear warheads and capable of threatening hardened targets. Depending on future munitions developments and the types of guidance systems incorporated in their designs, they could even-tually be accurate enough to permit the use of conventional warheads. With such warheads, highly accurate cruise missiles would pose a significant non-nuclear threat to US and NATO airfields and nuclear weapons in a non-nuclear conflict.

US Strategic Forces

By mid-1984, US strategic deterrent forces will consist of:
- 1,000 MINUTEMAN ICBMs,
- 33 TITAN ICBMs,
- 241 B-52G/H model bombers, plus about 23 aircraft undergoing maintenance and modification,
- 56 FB-111 bombers, plus some five aircraft undergoing maintenance and modification,
- 496 POSEIDON (C-3 and C-4) fleet ballistic launchers, and
- 120 TRIDENT fleet ballistic launchers.

The historic and continuing objective of US strategic forces is deterrence of nuclear and major conventional aggression against the United States and its Allies. This policy has preserved nuclear peace for over 38 years and, in sharp contrast to the Soviet priority accorded nuclear warfighting, is based on the conviction of all postwar American administrations that there could be no winners in a nuclear conflict. Rather, US deterrence policy seeks to maintain the situation where any potential aggressor sees little to gain and much to lose in initiating hostilities against the United States or its Allies. In turn, the maintenance of peace through nuclear deterrence provides the vital opportunity to realize a complementary and constant US goal of eliminating nuclear weapons from the arsenals of all states.

To realize these deterrence objectives requires the development, deployment and maintenance of strategic forces whose size and characteristics clearly indicate to an opponent that he cannot achieve his politico-military objectives either through employment of nuclear weapons or through political coercion based on nuclear advantages. Despite these pressing military requirements, the 1970s saw the United States exhibit restraint in modernizing its strategic forces. This was done to promote what was hoped to be significant progress in SALT negotiations. As a result, the United States did not introduce any new

ICBMs, SLBMs, SSBN classes or heavy strategic bombers in the 1972 to 1978 period. The United States did introduce the Short-Range Attack Missile (SRAM) to assist strategic bombers in penetrating the extensive and growing Soviet air defenses. A limited number, 66, of FB-111 shorter-range bombers were also deployed in the 1969-70 period. These developments were required to maintain the effectiveness of our bomber force in response to the Soviet air defense improvements.

The result of the asymmetry in US and Soviet modernization programs has been to erode the perception of US deterrent capability, and its continuation could weaken US ability to maintain peace. To preclude such a possibility, to restore the real and perceived deterrent capability of the United States and to resolve the problems associated with aging US forces, the President has initiated and the Congress has supported a comprehensive and integrated strategic modernization program. This program includes:

• deployment of more survivable and effective command, control and communications systems,
• development of the new TRIDENT-II submarine-launched ballistic missile and continued procurement of TRIDENT-Class submarines,
• procurement of 100 B-1B bombers in the near-term and deployment of the Advanced Technology Bomber for the 1990s,
• modernization of selected B-52 bombers and introduction of air-launched cruise missiles into the force,
• deployment of 100 new PEACE-KEEPER (MX) land-based missiles in MINUTEMAN silos beginning in 1986, and
• development of a new, small, single-warhead ICBM.

Strategic Defense

Strategic defenses are vital to the overall Soviet strategy for nuclear war. As noted above, the operations of Soviet defensive and attack forces are closely coupled; attack strategies are geared in large part to the reduction of the defensive burden. In the Soviet concept of a layered defense, effectiveness is achieved through multiple types of defensive capabilities compensating for shortcomings in individual systems and for the likelihood that neither offensive strikes nor any one layer of defense will stop all attacking weapons. The Soviets have made major improvements in their deployed strategic defenses and have invested heavily in ABM-related development.

Early Warning

Current Systems and Force Levels. The Soviets maintain the world's most extensive early warning system for both ballistic missile and air defense. Their operational ballistic missile early-warning system includes a launch detection satellite network, over-the-horizon radars and a series of large phased-array radars located primarily on the periphery of the USSR. Their early-warning air surveillance system is composed of an extensive network of ground-based radars linked operationally with those of their Warsaw Pact Allies.

The current Soviet launch detection satellite network is capable of providing about 30 minutes warning of any US ICBM launch, and of determining the area from which it originated. The two over-the-horizon radars the Soviets have directed at the US ICBM fields also could provide them with 30 minutes warning of an ICBM strike launched from the United States, but with somewhat less precision than the satellite network. Working together, these two early-warning systems can provide more reliable warning than either working alone.

The next layer of operational ballistic missile early warning consists of 11 large HEN HOUSE detection and tracking radars at six locations on the periphery of the USSR. These radars can distinguish the size of an attack, confirm the warning from the satellite and over-the-horizon radar systems and provide some target-tracking data in support of ABM deployments.

Current Soviet air surveillance radar deployments include more than 7,000 radars of various types located at about 1,200 sites. These deployments provide virtually complete coverage at medium to high altitudes over the USSR and in some areas extends hundreds of kilometers beyond the borders. Limited coverage against low-altitude targets is concentrated in the western USSR and in high-priority areas elsewhere. Since 1983, the Soviets have begun to deploy two new air surveillance radars. These radars assist in the early warning of cruise missile and bomber attacks and enhance air defense electronic warfare capabilities.

Force Developments. Since last year, an additional new large phased-array radar for ballistic missile early warning and target-tracking has been discovered under construction in Siberia. This brings to six the number of such radars operational or under construction in the USSR. This new radar closes the final gap in the combined HEN HOUSE and new large-phased array radar early-warning

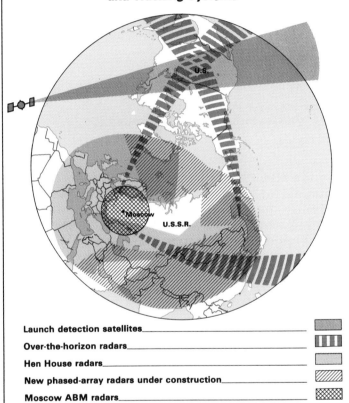

Coverage of Ballistic Missile Detection and Tracking Systems

Launch detection satellites
Over-the-horizon radars
Hen House radars
New phased-array radars under construction
Moscow ABM radars

and tracking network. Together, this radar and the five others like it form an arc of coverage from the Kola Peninsula in the northwest, around Siberia, to the Caucasus in the southwest. HEN HOUSE coverage completes the circle. The newly identified radar almost certainly violates the 1972 ABM Treaty in that it is not located on the periphery of the Soviet Union nor is it pointed outward as required by the Treaty. The complete network of these radars, which could provide target tracking data for ABM deployments beyond Moscow, probably will be operational by the late 1980s.

The Soviets may establish a network of satellites in geostationary orbit designed to provide timely indications of SLBM launches. Such a network could be operational by the end of the decade.

The USSR has a strong research and development program to produce new early warning and other air surveillance radars, as well as to improve existing systems. More than 20 types of these radars are currently in development. In addition, the Soviets are continuing to deploy improved air surveillance data systems that can rapidly pass data from outlying radars through the air surveillance network to ground-controlled intercept sites and SAM command posts. These systems will continue to be deployed until all areas are equipped with them.

Ballistic Missile Defense

Current Systems and Force Levels. The Soviets maintain around Moscow the world's only operational ABM system. This system is intended to afford a layer of defense for Soviet civil and military command authorities in the Moscow environs during a nuclear war rather than blanket protection for the city itself. Since 1980, the Soviets have been upgrading and expanding this system within the limits of the 1972 ABM Treaty.

The original single-layer Moscow ABM system included 64 reloadable above-ground launchers at four complexes for the GALOSH ABM-1B, six TRY ADD guidance and engagement radars at each complex and the DOG HOUSE and CAT HOUSE target-tracking radars south of Moscow. The Soviets are upgrading this system to the 100 launchers permitted under the Treaty. When completed, the new system will be a two-layer defense composed of silo-based long-range modified GALOSH interceptors designed to engage targets outside the atmosphere; silo-based high-acceleration interceptors designed to engage targets within the atmosphere; associated engagement and guidance radars; and a new large radar at Pushkino designed to control ABM engagements. The silo-based launchers may be reloadable. The new Moscow defenses are likely to reach fully operational status in the late 1980s.

Force Developments. The USSR has an improving potential for large-scale deployment of modernized ABM defenses well beyond the 100-launcher ABM Treaty limits. Widespread

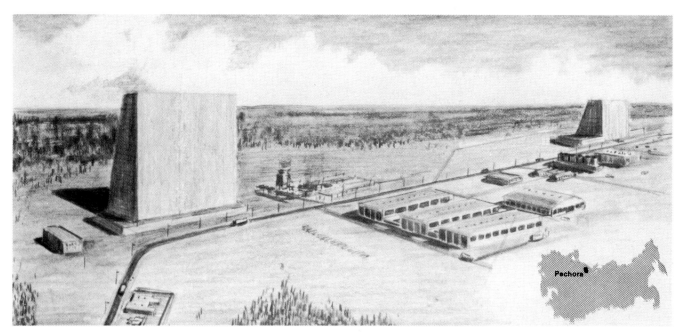

The receiver and transmitter of the large phased-array, early-warning and ballistic missile target-tracking radar at Pechora. An identical radar in the Central USSR almost certainly violates the 1972 ABM Treaty.

ABM deployment to protect important target areas in the USSR could be accomplished within the next 10 years. The Soviets have developed a rapidly deployable ABM system for which sites could be built in months instead of years. A typical site would consist of engagement radars, guidance radars, above-ground launchers and the high-acceleration interceptor. The new, large phased-array radars under construction in the USSR along with the HEN HOUSE, DOG HOUSE, CAT HOUSE and possibly the Pushkino radars appear to be designed to provide support for such a widespread ABM defense system. The Soviets seem to have placed themselves in a position to field relatively quickly a nationwide ABM system should they decide to do so.

In addition, the Soviets are deploying one surface-to-air missile system, the SA-10, and are flight-testing another, the mobile SA-X-12. The SA-X-12 is both a tactical SAM and antitactical ballistic missile. Both the SA-10 and SA-X-12 may have the potential to intercept some types of US strategic ballistic missiles as well. These systems could, if properly supported, add significant point-target coverage to a wide-spread ABM deployment.

Soviet-directed energy development programs involve future ABM as well as antisatellite and air-defense weapons concepts.

By the late 1980s, the Soviets could have prototypes for ground-based lasers for ballistic missile defense. The many difficulties in fielding an operational system will require much development time, and initial operational deployment is not likely in this century.

Ground- and space-based particle beam weapons for ballistic missile defense will be more difficult to develop than lasers. Nevertheless, the Soviets have a vigorous program underway for particle beam development and could have a prototype space-based system ready for testing in the late 1990s.

Antisatellite Systems

Current Systems and Force Levels. Since 1971, the Soviets have had the capability to attack satellites in near-earth orbit with a ground-based orbital interceptor. Using a radar sensor and a pellet-type warhead, the interceptor can attack a target in various orbits during its first two revolutions. An intercept during the first orbit would reduce the time available for a target satellite to take evasive action. The interceptor can reach targets orbiting at more than 5,000 kilometers, but it probably is intended for high priority satellites at lower altitudes. The antisatellite interceptor is launched from Tyuratam where two launch pads and storage space for additional

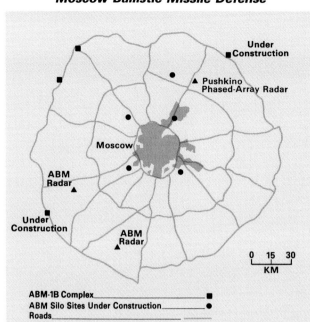

GALOSH anti-ballistic missile interceptors fitted on 64 surface launchers around Moscow, above left, are being replaced by silo-based exoatmospheric and endoatmospheric ABMs, shown during launch sequence at bottom.

interceptors and launch vehicles are available. Several interceptors could be launched each day from each of the pads. In addition to the orbital interceptor, the Soviets have two ground-based test lasers that could be used against satellites. The Soviets also have the technological capability to conduct electronic warfare against space systems.

Force Developments. Emerging directed energy technologies are seen by the Soviets as offering greater promise for future anti-satellite application than further development of orbital interceptors equipped with conventional warheads. The Soviets could deploy antisatellite lasers to several ground sites in the next 10 years or they could deploy laser-

Chapter II Forces for Global Warfare

This directed-energy R&D site at the Sary Shagan proving ground in the central USSR could provide some anti-satellite capabilities today and possibly ABM prototype testing in the future.

equipped satellites either available for launch on command or maintained in orbit, or could deploy both. Such systems would have significant advantages over a conventional orbital interceptor. These include longer-range, multi-shot capabilities and a greater capacity to overcome the target's defensive measures.

The Soviets could test a prototype laser antisatellite weapon as soon the late 1980s. Initial operational capability could be achieved between the early- and mid-1990s.

Since the early 1970s, the Soviets have had a research program to explore the technical feasibility of a particle beam weapon in space. A prototype space-based particle beam weapon intended only to disrupt satellite electronic equipment could be tested in the early 1990s. One designed to destroy the satellites could be tested in space in the mid-1990s.

Air Defense

Current Systems and Force Levels. The Soviets have deployed massive strategic air defense forces that currently have excellent capabilities against aircraft flying at medium and high altitudes but much less capability against low-flying aircraft and cruise missiles. Soviet air defenses, however, are in the initial stages of a major overhaul geared entirely to fielding an integrated air defense system much more capable of low-altitude op-

erations. This overhaul includes the partial integration of strategic and tactical air defenses; the upgrading of early-warning and air surveillance capabilities; the deployment of more efficient data transmission systems; and the development and initial deployment of

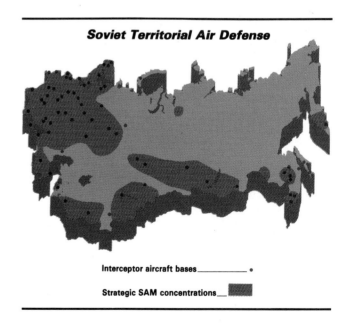

Soviet Territorial Air Defense

Interceptor aircraft bases_____ •

Strategic SAM concentrations__ [■■■]

new aircraft, associated air-to-air missiles, surface-to-air missiles and an airborne warning and control system (AWACS).

MiG-25/FOXBAT E Interceptor.

Currently, the Soviets have some 1,200 air defense interceptors and nearly 10,000 SAM launchers at over 900 sites dedicated to strategic territorial air defense. An additional 2,000 interceptors and some 1,800 tactical SAMs are deployed within the USSR's borders and could be made available for territorial defense.

Older FOXBAT aircraft are being upgraded to the FOXBAT E configuration giving them somewhat better look-down radar capabilities. More importantly, however, the new MiG-31/FOXHOUND interceptor, the first true look-down/shoot-down-capable aircraft in the Soviet inventory, is being introduced. The FOXHOUND aircraft is comparable in size to the US F-14. Over 50 of these aircraft are now operational.

The new multiple altitude SA-10 SAM, first deployed in 1980, is now operational at some 40 sites with nearly 350 launchers and four SA-10s per launcher. In addition, SA-5 deployment continues at a very slow pace within the USSR. The most significant SA-5 deployments have occurred outside the USSR in Eastern Europe, Mongolia and Syria.

Force Developments. Virtually all of the Soviet air defense development programs now underway are geared to overcoming a long-standing vulnerability to low-altitude air attack. Two new fighter interceptors—the Su-27/FLANKER and the MiG-29/FULCRUM—have true look-down/shoot-down capabilities. The FULCRUM is a single-seat, twin engine fighter similar in size to the US F-16. It was first deployed earlier this year. The FLANKER is larger than the FULCRUM and is about the same size as the US F-15. It, too, is a

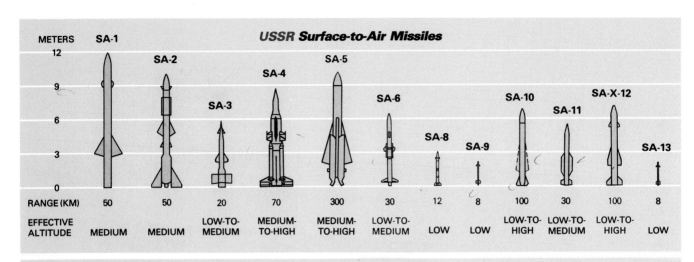

USSR *Surface-to-Air Missiles*

	SA-1	SA-2	SA-3	SA-4	SA-5	SA-6	SA-8	SA-9	SA-10	SA-11	SA-X-12	SA-13
RANGE (KM)	50	50	20	70	300	30	12	8	100	30	100	8
EFFECTIVE ALTITUDE	MEDIUM	MEDIUM	LOW-TO-MEDIUM	MEDIUM-TO-HIGH	MEDIUM-TO-HIGH	LOW-TO-MEDIUM	LOW	LOW	LOW-TO-HIGH	LOW-TO-MEDIUM	LOW-TO-HIGH	LOW

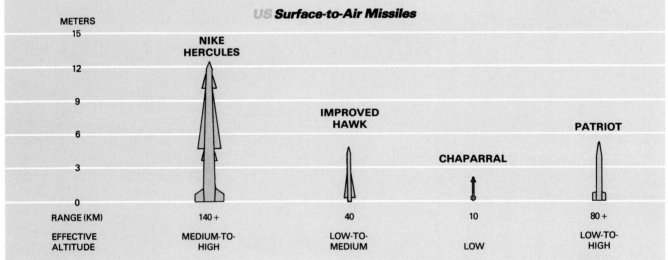

US *Surface-to-Air Missiles*

	NIKE HERCULES	IMPROVED HAWK	CHAPARRAL	PATRIOT
RANGE (KM)	140 +	40	10	80 +
EFFECTIVE ALTITUDE	MEDIUM-TO-HIGH	LOW-TO-MEDIUM	LOW	LOW-TO-HIGH

single-seat, twin-engine fighter, and it could be operationally deployed this year or next. Both have been designed to be highly maneuverable, air-to-air combat aircraft.

These two aircraft and the FOXHOUND are likely to operate under certain circumstances with the new Il-76/MAINSTAY Airborne Warning and Control Systems (AWACS) aircraft. The MAINSTAY will substantially improve Soviet capabilities for early warning and air combat command and control. It will provide the Soviets with the capability over land and water to detect aircraft and cruise missile targets flying at low altitudes. The MAINSTAY could be used to help direct fighter operations over European and Asian battlefields and to enhance air surveillance and defense of the USSR. Four of these aircraft have been built. The MAINSTAY should be operational this year; an annual production rate of about five aircraft is likely.

The three new Soviet fighter-interceptors

are equipped with two new air-to-air missiles—the AA-9 designed for the FOXHOUND and the AA-X-10 designed for the FULCRUM and the FLANKER. The AA-9 is a long-range missile that can be used against low-flying aircraft; the AA-X-10 is a medium-range missile with similar capabilities.

In keeping with their drive toward mobility as a means of weapons survival, the Soviets are developing a mobile version of the SA-10 SAM. This mobile version could be used to support Soviet theater forces, but, perhaps more importantly, if deployed with the territorial defense forces, it would allow the Soviets to change the location of those SA-10s in the USSR. The mobile SA-10 could be operational by 1985.

The Soviets have efforts underway to develop at least three types of high-energy laser weapons for air defense. These include lasers intended for defense of high-value strategic targets in the USSR, those for point defense of

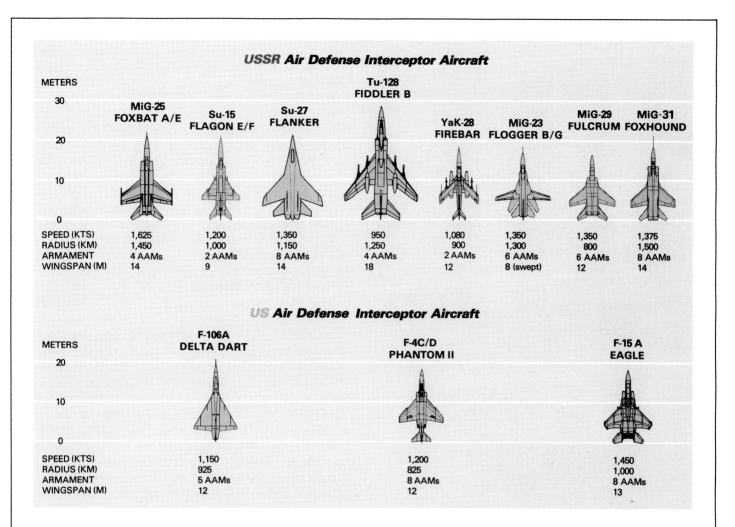

USSR Air Defense Interceptor Aircraft

	MiG-25 FOXBAT A/E	Su-15 FLAGON E/F	Su-27 FLANKER	Tu-128 FIDDLER B	YaK-28 FIREBAR	MiG-23 FLOGGER B/G	MiG-29 FULCRUM	MiG-31 FOXHOUND
SPEED (KTS)	1,625	1,200	1,350	950	1,080	1,350	1,350	1,375
RADIUS (KM)	1,450	1,000	1,150	1,250	900	1,300	800	1,500
ARMAMENT	4 AAMs	2 AAMs	8 AAMs	4 AAMs	2 AAMs	6 AAMs	6 AAMs	8 AAMs
WINGSPAN (M)	14	9	14	18	12	8 (swept)	12	14

US Air Defense Interceptor Aircraft

	F-106A DELTA DART	F-4C/D PHANTOM II	F-15 A EAGLE
SPEED (KTS)	1,150	1,200	1,450
RADIUS (KM)	925	825	1,000
ARMAMENT	5 AAMs	8 AAMs	8 AAMs
WINGSPAN (M)	12	12	13

ships at sea and theater-forces air defense. Following past practice, the Soviets are likely to deploy air-defense lasers to complement rather than replace interceptors and SAMs. The territorial-defense laser is probably in at least the prototype stage of development and could be operational between the mid- to-late 1980s. It most likely will be deployed in conjunction with SAMs in a point defense role. Since the two systems would have different attributes and vulnerabilities, they would provide mutual support. The shipborne lasers probably will not be operational until after the end of the decade. The theater-force lasers may be operational sometime sooner and are likely to be capable of structurally damaging aircraft at close ranges and producing electro-optical and eye damage at greater distances.

In addition, the Soviets have underway a development program for an airborne laser. Assuming a successful development effort, limited initial deployment could begin in the early 1990s. Such a laser platform could have

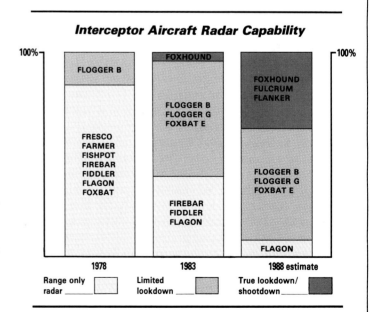

missions including antisatellite defense, protection of high-value airborne assets and cruise-missile defense.

The mobile SA-10 SAM will soon be operational.

Passive Defense

Soviet passive defense preparations have been underway in earnest for some 30 years, and have, over time, expanded from the protection of such vital entities as the national Party and government leadership and Armed Forces, to embrace the territorial leadership, national economy and general population. The Soviets regard passive defense as an essential ingredient of their overall military posture and their war planning. In conjunction with active forces, the Soviets plan for their passive defense program to ensure the survival and wartime continuity of:

• Soviet leadership,
• military command and control,
• war-supporting industrial production and services, and
• the essential workforce and protection of as much of the general population as possible.

As this program has expanded, elements of it have been designated by the Soviets as "civil defense." Use of this term in its normal Western context does not convey the full scope of Soviet Civil Defense.

Extensive planning for the transition of the entire State and economy to a wartime posture has been fundamental to Soviet passive defense preparations. The Soviet General Staff and Civil Defense officials have supervised the development of special organizations and procedures to implement quickly the transition to war and have emphasized the mobilization and protection of all national resources essential to the successful prosecution of war and recovery.

The senior Soviet military establishment has also supervised the 30-year program to construct hardened command posts and survivable communications for key military commanders and civilian managers at all levels of the Party and government. Likewise, protective hardening, dispersal and wartime production plans for Soviet industry have all been coordinated with the wartime requirements of the military and supervised by Civil Defense personnel. The protection of the general population through evacuation procedures and extensive sheltering in or near urban areas is the most visible aspect of the passive defense program.

Soviet Civil Defense Management. These passive defense programs reflect the Soviet concept of the system in its wartime mode. The wartime management system would be a militarized system of national administration in which peacetime government bodies become Civil Defense components under direct military subordination. This would extend to Soviet territorial administration at all levels and to specialized functional components such as industrial, transport, power and communications ministries. Soviet authorities at all levels would serve as uniformed chiefs of Civil Defense and command their respective organizations in a military capacity. Soviet Civil Defense thus serves both as a vehicle to administer peacetime preparations and training and as the infrastructure that would knit together civil and military bodies in their unified wartime management systems.

Continuity of Leadership Functions. Soviet commanders and managers at all levels of the Party and government are provided hardened alternate command posts located well away from urban centers. This comprehensive and redundant system, composed of more than 1,500 hardened facilities with special communications, is patterned after similar capabilities afforded the Armed Forces. More than 175,000 key personnel throughout the system are believed to be equipped with such alternate facilities in addition to the many deep bunkers and blast shelters in Soviet cities.

Stability of the Wartime Economy. Soviet passive defense efforts include measures to maintain essential production and services even during a nuclear war. Elaborate plans have been set for the full mobilization of the national economy in support of the war effort and the conversion to wartime production. Reserves of vital materials are maintained, many in hardened underground structures. Redundant industrial facilities have been built and are in active production. Industrial and other economic facilities have been equipped with blast shelters for the workforce, and detailed procedures have been developed for the relocation of selected plants and equipment. By ensuring the survival of essential workers, the Soviets intend to reconstitute vital production programs using those industrial components that can be redirected or salvaged after attack.

North American Defense Forces

US and Canadian interceptor forces assigned to the North American Aerospace Defense (NORAD) Command maintain continuous ground alert at sites around the periphery of the United States and Canada. Alert aircraft intercept and identify unknown intruders. In a crisis, the Air Force, Navy and Marine Corps would provide additional interceptors. Supported by AWACS aircraft, these forces could provide a limited defense against bomber attacks.

To meet the increasing Soviet bomber and ALCM threats, US interceptor squadrons assigned to NORAD are being equipped with newer, more advanced F-15 and F-16 aircraft. These modern fighters will provide a lookdown/shoot-down capability to detect and engage enemy bombers penetrating at low altitudes. The Canadians are upgrading their air defense forces with the CF-18. Joint US and Canadian programmed improvements to long-range surveillance include modern microwave radars for the Distant Early Warning line and over-the-horizon back-scatter radars looking east, west and south.

Soviet space-oriented military systems pose an unacceptable threat to the land, sea and air forces of the United States. Soviet satellites probably have the capability to support targeting of Soviet anti-ship cruise missiles launched against US surface ships. The US anti-satellite (ASAT) program, centering on the Air-Launched Miniature Vehicle, is part of our response to this and similar threats. At the same time, we are continuing to examine the potential basis for negotiating ASAT arms control agreements.

Finally, the United States has called for a research program to explore the possibility of strengthening deterrence by taking advantage of recent advances in technology that could, in the long term, provide an effective defense against ballistic missiles. The effort focuses on existing research programs in five technology areas that offer the greatest promise. Given the extensive Soviet efforts in this area, the US program is a prudent and necessary hedge against the possibility of unilateral Soviet deployment of an advanced system capable of effectively countering Western ballistic missiles. Such a unilateral Soviet deployment — added to the USSR's impressive air and passive defense capabilities — would jeopardize deterrence because the US would no longer be able to pose a credible threat of retaliation to a Soviet attack.

Nuclear Stockpiles

Since the first Soviet nuclear explosion on August 29, 1949, the Soviet stockpile of nuclear warheads has grown steadily, primarily in the area of offensive weapons. In contrast, the US stockpile was one-third higher in 1967 than it is today. In addition, as a result of two landmark NATO decisions in 1979 and 1983, the nuclear stockpile in Europe will decline by one-third from its 1979 level.

The USSR's nuclear weapons program has shown diversity and sophistication. Today, Soviet nuclear warheads include a full spectrum of fission and thermonuclear designs using uranium, plutonium and tritium, with weapons yields up to multimegaton. The preponderance of these weapons is assigned to strategic offensive forces. Because of MIRVing, the megatonnage in the Soviet arsenal leveled in the early seventies, and then began to drop. However, with the deployment of new

Chapter II Forces for Global Warfare

Soviet Military Power 1983 *reported the development of a small Soviet space plane. Shown at left and above is the recovery of a scale model of that plane after orbit and splash-down in the Indian Ocean.*

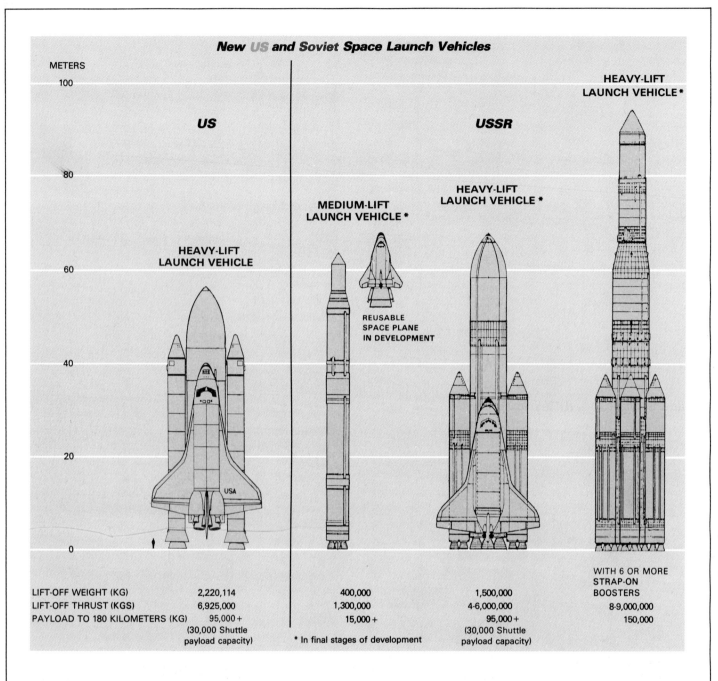

New US and Soviet Space Launch Vehicles

METERS

	US		**USSR**		

US — HEAVY-LIFT LAUNCH VEHICLE

USSR — MEDIUM-LIFT LAUNCH VEHICLE * (REUSABLE SPACE PLANE IN DEVELOPMENT)

USSR — HEAVY-LIFT LAUNCH VEHICLE *

USSR — HEAVY-LIFT LAUNCH VEHICLE * (WITH 6 OR MORE STRAP-ON BOOSTERS)

	US	USSR MEDIUM-LIFT	USSR HEAVY-LIFT	USSR HEAVY-LIFT
LIFT-OFF WEIGHT (KG)	2,220,114	400,000	1,500,000	
LIFT-OFF THRUST (KGS)	6,925,000	1,300,000	4-6,000,000	8-9,000,000
PAYLOAD TO 180 KILOMETERS (KG)	95,000+ (30,000 Shuttle payload capacity)	15,000+	95,000+ (30,000 Shuttle payload capacity)	150,000

* In final stages of development

nuclear weapons systems their stockpile megatonnage has again started to rise.

The Soviet nuclear energy and weapons development program and its associated industrial base are characterized by a highly centralized control structure. The ministry controlling nuclear weapons development and production is in charge of all nuclear materials, reactors and weapons research and development (R&D) as well as production. Since the ministry controls virtually all facilities related to the nuclear industry, reactor utilization can be unilaterally altered to satisfy military requirements, regardless of the military or commercial nature of the particular reactor facility.

Finally, during the past two decades, the number of workers and the amount of floor space of the Soviet nuclear weapons research and development facilities have exhibited constant growth. Manpower devoted to nuclear R&D probably exceeds 30,000 employees and is comprised of the best scientists, mathematicians, engineers and technicians Soviet academia can produce. Their R&D efforts are supported by an active nuclear test program conducted at the Novaya Zemlya and Semipalitinsk nuclear test sites.

The Soviet Space Program

Soviet Military Power 1983 outlined the expansion into space of the Soviet quest for military superiority. During the ensuing year, the Soviets have made progress toward their dual military objectives of global support to military forces and denial of enemy employment of space during wartime. In addition, progress has been made toward the two other key objectives of enhancing the influence and prestige of the USSR and contributing to the Soviet economy. There has been no change in the heavy Soviet emphasis on the military applications of space, reflecting their view, noted as early as two decades ago in the classified Soviet military publication, *Military Thought,* that "the mastering of space [is] a prerequisite for achieving victory in war."

Since last year, the Soviet developmental programs for providing a family of new space launch vehicles and reusable spacecraft suitable for military and civil purposes have come into sharper focus. Significant new launch and support facilities at Tyuratam are nearing completion. Some of these should be ready this year or next to support initial testing of new launch vehicles. These vehicles include a space transportation system (STS), that in many respects copies the design of the US space shuttle, a new heavy-lift launch vehicle based on the core rockets of the STS and a new medium-lift launch vehicle that is evidently designed for high launch rates. The new spacecraft include a space shuttle that differs from the US shuttle only in the respect that the main engines are not on the orbiter, a small space plane that could be a test vehicle or a scale version of a military space plane, and a space tug that would be used in space to move equipment and supplies from one orbit to another. The Soviet shuttle could be first tested in the mid-to-late 1980s. The space plane scale model has already been tested three times, and the space tug probably will reach operational status late in the 1980s.

In addition, the Soviets evidently intend to continue using their many types of operational space launch vehicles for at least another decade. This current family of vehicles, which supports a space effort of 100 or more launches per year, combined with the new generation of systems, indicates that the Soviets will be able by the mid- to-late 1980s to increase significantly their space program both in numbers and payload weight. In this

The SL-4 space launch vehicle is the workhorse of the current Soviet manned space program.

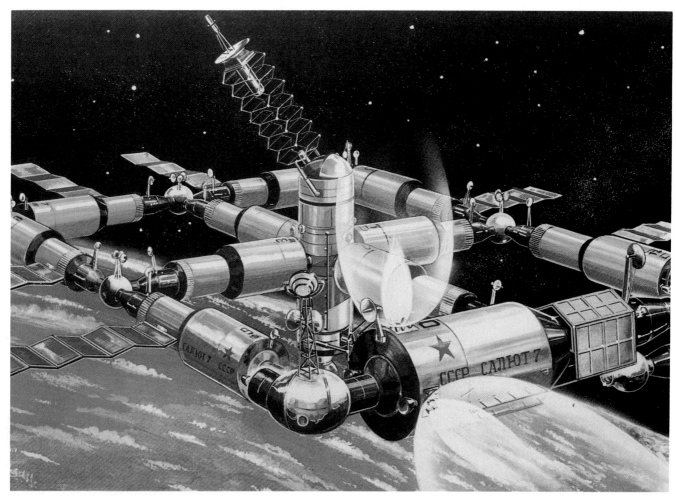

The Soviets have announced plans to have a large, permanently manned space station orbiting the earth in the 1990s. This station, which would serve military purposes, could appear as shown in this artist's depiction.

regard, the new heavy-lift vehicle is estimated to have the capability to place payloads weighing upwards of 330,000 pounds into low-earth orbit. This is about seven times more than the largest operational Soviet booster can deliver today, and about five times the maximum US capability. Despite the obvious civil and scientific uses to which these capabilities could be put, the Soviets will continue, as in the past, to devote most of their future space program to military purposes.

Military systems now account for more than 70 percent of Soviet space launches. Another 20 percent have combined military-civil application, with less than 10 percent devoted to purely civil/scientific activities. Very little of their effort is devoted to programs that have economic benefit.

The Soviets routinely conduct about four to five times as many space launches per year as

the United States. This is necessitated primarily by the shorter system lifetimes and poorer reliability of most Soviet satellites. The fact that they routinely operate this way in peacetime, however, gives them an inherently greater capability to increase rapidly the number of military satellites in orbit and to replace lost or damaged satellites as long as launch facilities are intact.

The US and USSR currently maintain about the same number of operational satellites in orbit, 110 to 120. The Soviet inventory of operational space systems provides the capability to perform the following military functions:

• reconnaissance and surveillance,
• command, control and communications,
• ICBM launch detection and attack warning,
• strategic and tactical targeting,

- navigational support,
- meteorological support, and
- antisatellite operations.

The Soviets have satellites that are designed to perform naval surveillance and targeting missions. These satellites are strictly military systems intended to support Soviet naval operations against large surface ships and other surface ship formations.

The Soviets have a deployed antisatellite weapon system that is capable of attacking satellites in low-to-medium earth orbits. The intercontinental warfare section of this chapter has addressed Soviet antisatellite and other space-oriented weapons programs in some detail. Recent Soviet proposals to ban all ASAT tests and future deployments of ASAT weapons are intended to put the United States at a disadvantage in this area. It is important to note that the proposed treaty does not prevent developing and deploying advanced ground-based weapons—such as high energy lasers—that could be used in an antisatellite role.

Estimated Dollar Costs of the Soviet Space Program *

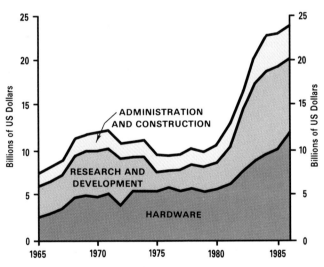

* Estimates represent cost in constant 1981 dollars for the US to replicate known Soviet development and procurement of space systems. Launch and operation costs are not included.

The Soviets continue to pursue their manned space programs maintaining in orbit the SALYUT space station, which is manned during most of the year. This gives the Soviets the capability to perform a variety of functions from space, including military R&D and the use of man to augment their other reconnaissance and surveillance efforts. A larger, permanently manned space station, expected during the next decade, will significantly increase their in-orbit operations capabilities. This station could be used as a stepping stone to interplanetary exploration and the establishment of bases on other planetary bodies. The Soviets, however, are more likely to use such a station to perform command and control, reconnaissance and targeting functions. During wartime, it could perform these functions and more offensively oriented missions as well. The Soviets believe in the military utility of maintaining cosmonauts in orbit. Over the next 10 years, therefore, the Soviets are likely to develop primarily for military purposes:

- a permanently manned SKYLAB-size space station to be operational in the next 2-3 years with a 6- to 12-person crew, and
- a very large modular space station, to be operational by the early- to-mid-1990s, which could house as many as 100 personnel.

By all measures, the Soviet level of effort devoted to space in the 1980s is increasing significantly over the activities noted in the 1970s. The projected yearly rate of growth of the Soviet space program is expected to outpace both the annual rate of growth in overall Soviet military spending and that of the Soviet gross national product (GNP) for a number of years to come.

The Soviets have embarked upon a long-term, broad-based effort to expand their operational military capability in space. A major Soviet objective is to expand warfighting capability in space and achieve a measure of superiority in that arena. Their technological base is strengthening and is being enhanced by technology transfer from the West. Their launch capability is increasing with the development of new facilities and booster systems. They continue to operate the world's only operational antisatellite system, while they test and develop more sophisticated space weaponry. It is clear the Soviets are striving to integrate their space systems with the rest of their Armed Forces to ensure superior military capabilities in all arenas.

Chapter III
Theater Forces

Over the past two decades, Soviet forces for theater warfare have been steadily expanded and upgraded in every category of weapons systems. Soviet ground force divisions have been enlarged and equipped with the most modern tanks, artillery and helicopters. Soviet naval forces continue to receive larger and more lethal ships and submarines. Soviet air forces are being modernized with high-performance aircraft while theater missile forces receive more accurate systems with greater range and throwweight. In addition to these force enhancements, Soviet military planners adapt tactics to the capability of new systems and changing political objectives.

The Soviets envision as many as three main theaters for the Eurasian land mass: Western, Southern and Far Eastern, each with a set of political objectives affecting military operations within the theater. More importantly in planning for such military operations the Soviets divide a theater, for operational-command and strategic planning purposes, into theaters of military operations (TVDs). Soviet planning for the Western theater, encompassing all of Europe, envisions three continental TVDs—Northwestern, Western and Southwestern—and two maritime, Arctic and Atlantic. This organizational concept enables military planners to formulate military strategy and tactics to achieve political objectives in the geographic region, taking into consideration the capabilities of the missiles, aircraft, ships and ground forces at their disposal. The same planning process occurs for Soviet objectives in the Southern and Far Eastern Theaters.

In the Western TVD, Soviet war aims would be to defeat NATO and occupy Western

To counter high-performance aircraft and theater warfare missiles, the missiles of the new SA-X-12 air defense system are fired from mobile launchers, accompanied by reload vehicles and supported by target-tracking and fire control radars. The SA-X-12 is part of the USSR's continuing large investment in strategic and tactical defenses.

Soviet Theater Forces

BALTIC FLEET

PRINCIPAL SURFACE COMBATANTS	42
OTHER COMBATANT SHIPS	99
COMBATANT CRAFT	245
AUXILIARIES	160
SUBMARINES	32
NAVAL AVIATION	275
NAVAL INFANTRY BRIGADE	

30 SOVIET DIVISIONS
56 NON-SOVIET WARSAW PACT DIVISIONS

WESTERN THEATER*

65 DIVISIONS
TACTICAL AIRCRAFT 3,600
SS-20 243
SS-4 224

☆ Moscow

STRATEGIC RESERVE MILITARY DISTRICTS
17 DIVISIONS

NORTHERN FLEET

PRINCIPAL SURFACE COMBATANTS	78
OTHER COMBATANT SHIPS	71
COMBATANT CRAFT	60
AUXILIARIES	205
SUBMARINES	151**
NAVAL AVIATION	425
NAVAL INFANTRY BRIGADE	

FAR EAST THEATER

FAR EAST

52 DIVISIONS
TACTICAL AIRCRAFT 1,820
SS-20 135

INCLUDES FORCES LOCATED IN MONGOLIA

BLACK SEA FLEET/CASPIAN FLOTILLA

PRINCIPAL SURFACE COMBATANTS	77
OTHER COMBATANT SHIPS	85
COMBATANT CRAFT	215
AUXILIARIES	180
SUBMARINES	24
NAVAL AVIATION	405
NAVAL INFANTRY BRIGADE	

SOUTHERN THEATER

SOVIET SOUTHERN FORCES

30 DIVISIONS
TACTICAL AIRCRAFT 860

INCLUDES FORCES LOCATED IN AFGHANISTAN

PACIFIC FLEET

PRINCIPAL SURFACE COMBATANTS	89
OTHER COMBATANT SHIPS	112
COMBATANT CRAFT	245
AUXILIARIES	235
SUBMARINES	102**
NAVAL AVIATION	440
NAVAL INFANTRY DIVISION	

* The Western Theater includes what would become, in wartime, the Northwestern, Western, and Southwestern Theaters of Military Operations (TVDs). The Southern and Far Eastern theaters would also form TVDs—a total of five continental TVDs.

** Excludes DELTA, YANKEE and TYPHOON-Class Submarines

Europe before it could be reinforced. The Soviets plan for a very rapid, combined arms operation to reach the Atlantic in the shortest time possible. Soviet ground formations hope to achieve a rate of advance of up to 100 kilometers per day. Formations that met stiff resistance would be rapidly reinforced by second echelon forces. The Soviets plan to employ Operational Maneuver Groups (OMGs) in sharp thrusts to destroy enemy forces in depth.

Soviet ground formations are provided with attack helicopters for close air support to maintain rapid momentum. Additionally, transport helicopters and aircraft are provided to inject airmobile and air-assault units rapidly from 50 to 100 kilometers ahead of a main attack to disrupt the enemy, seize key terrain and to support operations by OMGs. Soviet special purpose forces, SPETSNAZ, would be employed throughout Western Europe for reconnaissance, to disrupt communications, destroy bridges, seize choke points and direct attacking aircraft to prime targets. Soviet air, missile and naval forces would all be employed in support of these operations.

The Soviets recognize the importance of nuclear weapons, which can have a direct influence on the course and outcome of a war. They also recognize that the war aims can only be achieved by the combined operations of all forces in a systematic fashion controlled by a centralized strategic command authority. Planning is constantly revised to reflect shifting political objectives as well as the introduction of more capable weapons systems.

In considering the possibility that a conventional conflict in Europe might escalate, the Soviets have developed extensive plans either to preempt a NATO nuclear strike by launching a massive attack, or to launch a massive first strike against prime NATO targets. Soviet ballistic missiles, rockets, nuclear-capable aircraft and artillery could all be employed in a massed strike against a set of targets beginning at the battle line and extending to the depth of the theater. Soviet ground forces have been trained and equipment developed for sustained operations in a nuclear environment. Even after a nuclear exchange, the Soviets expect they could continue their rapid combined arms offensive against NATO.

Soviet Missiles

With the initial deployment of the SS-20 LRINF missile in 1977, the Soviets launched a concerted effort to modernize and expand their intermediate-range nuclear force. Each SS-20 carries three MIRVed warheads, thereby providing a significant force expansion factor. To date, 378 SS-20s have been deployed, of which some 243 are opposite NATO. The mobility of the SS-20 system enables both on- and off-road operation. As a result, the survivability of the SS-20 is greatly enhanced because detecting and targeting them is difficult when they are field deployed. Further, the SS-20 launcher has the capability of being reloaded and refired; the Soviets stockpile refire missiles. The SS-20s also have very significant increases in accuracy and reaction time over the older SS-4s and SS-5s.

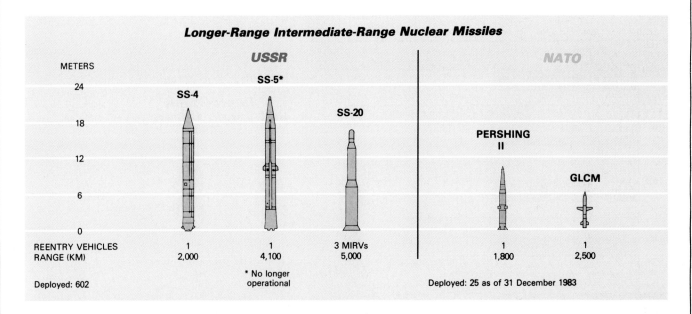

Longer-Range Intermediate-Range Nuclear Missiles

	USSR				NATO	
	SS-4	SS-5*	SS-20		PERSHING II	GLCM
REENTRY VEHICLES	1	1	3 MIRVs		1	1
RANGE (KM)	2,000	4,100	5,000		1,800	2,500

Deployed: 602

* No longer operational

Deployed: 25 as of 31 December 1983

The mobile SS-20 LRINF missile launchers—with three nuclear warheads on each missile and with a reload for each launcher—are targeted against Western Europe, China and Japan.

Force expansion is continuing, and the number of deployed SS-20 launchers could increase by at least 50 percent by the late 1980s. In addition to the SS-20 force, the Soviets still maintain some 224 SS-4 LRINF missiles. All of these older missiles are located in the western USSR opposite NATO. By the end of 1983, all SS-5 LRINF missiles were being retired.

Soviet theater nuclear capability has undergone other significant improvements, evident from the increased numbers, types, sophistication, accuracy and yields of tactical missiles including the SS-21, SS-22 and SS-23. The SS-21 is a division-level system that is replacing the older FROG-7. It has a range of about 120 kilometers compared to the FROG-7's range of about 70 kilometers, and is more accurate and reliable, thus enabling greater

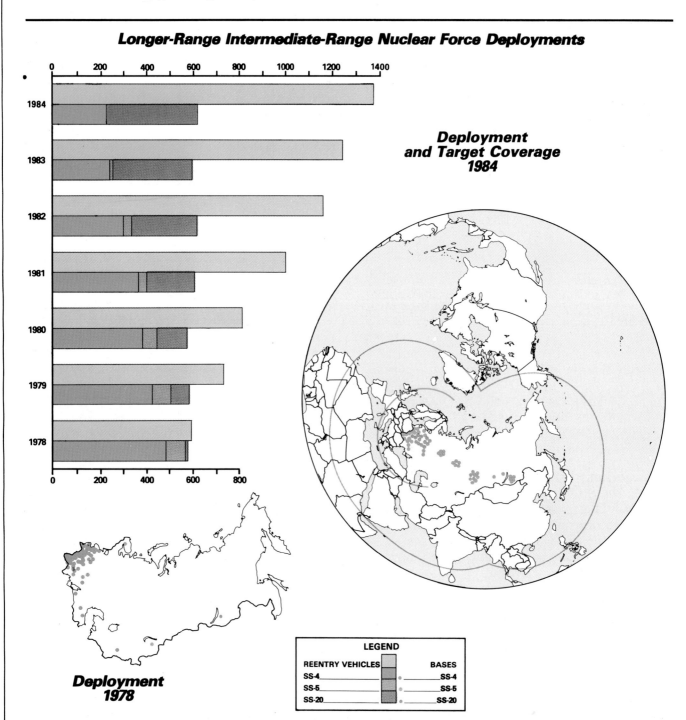

Longer-Range Intermediate-Range Nuclear Force Deployments

Deployment and Target Coverage 1984

Deployment 1978

LEGEND

REENTRY VEHICLES   BASES

SS-4   SS-4

SS-5   SS-5

SS-20   SS-20

targeting flexibility and deeper strikes.

The SCUD, normally deployed in brigades at army and front level, is expected to be replaced by the SS-23, a tactical surface-to-surface missile with improved accuracy and a range of 500 kilometers, versus the SCUD's 300 kilometers.

The SS-12/SCALEBOARD missile, with a range of about 900 kilometers, is expected to be replaced by the SS-22 of similar range but greater accuracy.

Even with the introduction of these new systems, Soviet efforts to develop newer and more accurate and reliable missiles continue.

SS-1C/SCUD B missiles on transporter-erector-launchers.

The Soviets are likely to improve the SS-20. They already have in advanced testing, and nearing deployment, ground-, air- and sea-launched long-range cruise missiles. There is evidence they are developing a new Short-Range Ballistic Missile, possibly for deployment later this decade or in the early 1990s.

In addition to the land-based theater missile forces, the Soviets still maintain and operate 13 GOLF II and two HOTEL II-Class ballistic missile submarines. Each submarine is equipped with three SS-N-5 SLBMs. Six GOLF II units are based in the Baltic where they continue to pose an effective threat to most of Europe, while the remaining seven submarines patrol the Sea of Japan where they could be employed against targets in the Far East.

US Non-Strategic Forces

In contrast to the Soviet modernization and build-up of its non-strategic nuclear force posture in Europe, the United States and its NATO Allies have exercised restraint.

In October 1983, NATO decided to withdraw 1,400 nuclear warheads from Europe. This decision will bring to 2,400 the total number of warheads to be removed from Europe since 1979. The earlier withdrawal of 1,000 warheads was mandated when NATO made its 1979 dual-track decision to modernize longer-range intermediate-range nuclear forces and to pursue arms control negotiations with the Soviet Union. Moreover, the current reduction will reduce NATO's nuclear stockpile to the lowest level in over 20 years and will not be affected by deployment of new LRINF missiles, because one warhead will be removed for each PERSHING II missile or ground-launched cruise missile (GLCM) warhead deployed.

The initial deployment of PERSHING II and ground-launched cruise missiles began in Europe in late 1983. Deployment will continue until 1988 when 108 PERSHING II and 464 GLCMs will be in place, unless a US-Soviet agreement that eliminates or limits the global number of LRINF missiles on both sides is concluded. The deployment of US PERSHING II and ground-launched cruise missiles responds to the Soviet LRINF missile threat to Europe.

As the US PERSHING IIs replace the shorter-range PERSHING Is, and Soviet SS-23s replace the SCUDs in Europe, the Soviet Union will at least maintain its substantial numerical superiority in shorter-range non-strategic nuclear missiles while improving the qualitative characteristics of its forces. The USSR also possesses a significant numerical advantage in INF aircraft and is reducing the qualitative advantage NATO has enjoyed, despite NATO's INF aircraft modernization program, which consists of the replacement of older aircraft with the F-16 and TORNADO.

Short-range nuclear forces (SNF) consist of tube artillery and missiles of much shorter range than INF missiles. The balance in SNF artillery, traditionally an area of NATO advantage, also has shifted dramatically in favor of the Soviets in recent years. The Soviets have achieved parity in overall numbers of SNF and continue to have a substantial advantage in the category of short-range missiles, giving them more flexibility in the employment of SNF.

Soviet Tactical Air Defense Missiles

The air defense of the Soviet forces has grown from earlier generation antiaircraft gun defenses to the modern antiaircraft guns and surface-to-air missile systems of today. Since each unit must be able to defend itself, air defense is the responsibility of all levels of command.

Soviet doctrine for air defense calls for the denial of the airspace over and adjacent to the battle area. To satisfy this requirement, the Soviets have developed a mixture of weapons that achieve coverage from the surface to very high altitudes. Current tactical air defense systems and their echelon assignments are:

System	Echelon
SA-7a and 7b	Company/Battalion
SA-14	
SA-9	Regiment
SA-13	
ZSU-23-4	
SA-6a and 6b	Division
SA-8a and 8b	
SA-11	
SA-4a and 4b	Front/Army

In their modernization program, the Soviets are seeking to improve surveillance, identification, target tracking, fire control, firepower and the ability to operate in all environments. This effort involves advances in such areas as radars, electro-optics, laser/directed energy technology and Identification Friend or Foe (IFF) systems.

The Soviets are also developing an advanced tactical air defense system, SA-X-12, to augment or replace the SA-4 in SAM brigades at the front level. This system is capable of engaging high-performance aircraft and short-range ballistic missiles like the US LANCE. It may also be used to attempt to intercept longer-range INF missiles. This system, like some other systems assigned to Soviet theater forces, could be used for territorial defense.

US Tactical Air Defense Systems

US and Allied tactical air defenses include several new weapons. The STINGER, with improved infrared-seeker guidance systems, a man-portable, surface-to-air missile system developed to replace the REDEYE. Two new systems, PATRIOT and the SGT YORK Division Air Defense Gun, will increase the Army's air defense capabilities against a variety of aircraft approaching at varying altitudes. PATRIOT will replace NIKE-HERCULES and the Improved HAWK as the principal theater-level SAM for defense against aircraft at high or medium altitudes and will be deployed in Europe beginning in 1984. The SGT YORK will give the Army a longer-range, all-weather, higher kill-probability weapon to protect armored and mechanized units. Beginning in 1985, the SGT YORK will replace the VULCAN gun system.

Soviet Air Forces

The reorganization of the command and control structure for Soviet air assets, which began in the late 1970s, is the most significant

Soviet air defense is comprised of a number of complementary systems, including fixed and mobile SAMs and air defense guns. Shown at left, the SA-4/GANEF mobile SAM and, at right, the ZSU-23-4 self-propelled antiaircraft gun.

event in the last two decades in the development of Soviet air power. It occurred as part of the general reorganization of Soviet military forces and is a result of the new emphasis on TVDs as the basic level of military operations in a future war.

The reorganization resulted in a streamlined organization due to the merger of strategic and tactical air and air defense assets in most land border areas of the USSR. The air defense (APVO) interceptor regiments in these areas were resubordinated from PVO Strany to the Soviet Air Forces. They became part of a new structure, the "Air Forces of the Military District," which also includes most of the assets of the former tactical air armies. The Air Forces of an MD include all air assets in their geographic area (excluding Strategic Aviation and transport assets). These assets can be used either offensively or defensively, as the situation requires. The new structure improves defensive capabilities, but its most

significant impact is on the capability to conduct massed offensive air operations in the various TVDs. The Soviets have probably been striving toward such a structure since the 1960s, and technological advances in weapon systems and in command, control and communications have finally made its implementation possible.

The Soviet Air Forces are currently adapting to their new organizational structure and to new weapon systems. Over the next few years, they will be settling more firmly into the reorganized structure and streamlining command and control links. There will be continued experimentation in tactics and training at all levels, as new roles and missions are more clearly defined.

Tactical Aviation: As a result of the reorganization, Soviet Air Forces of the Military Districts (MDs) now provide tactical air support to frontal operations. The missions assigned to the Air Forces of the MDs have

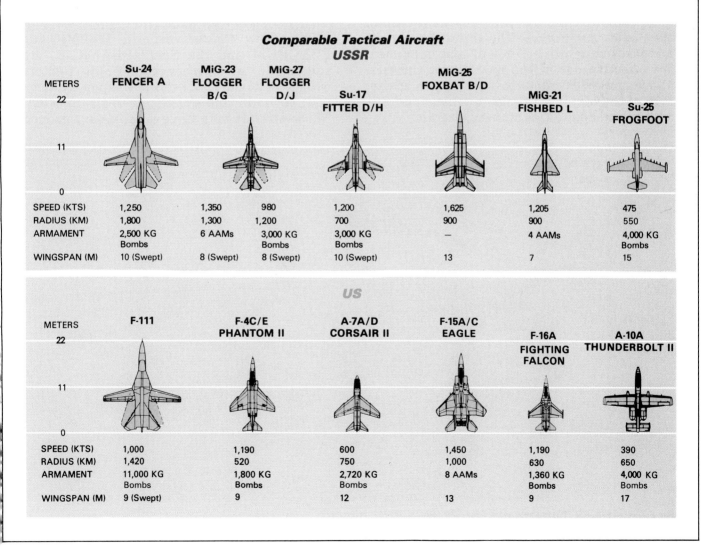

Comparable Tactical Aircraft

USSR

METERS	Su-24 FENCER A	MiG-23 FLOGGER B/G	MiG-27 FLOGGER D/J	Su-17 FITTER D/H	MiG-25 FOXBAT B/D	MiG-21 FISHBED L	Su-25 FROGFOOT
SPEED (KTS)	1,250	1,350	980	1,200	1,625	1,205	475
RADIUS (KM)	1,800	1,300	1,200	700	900	900	550
ARMAMENT	2,500 KG Bombs	6 AAMs	3,000 KG Bombs	3,000 KG Bombs	—	4 AAMs	4,000 KG Bombs
WINGSPAN (M)	10 (Swept)	8 (Swept)	8 (Swept)	10 (Swept)	13	7	15

US

METERS	F-111	F-4C/E PHANTOM II	A-7A/D CORSAIR II	F-15A/C EAGLE	F-16A FIGHTING FALCON	A-10A THUNDERBOLT II
SPEED (KTS)	1,000	1,190	600	1,450	1,190	390
RADIUS (KM)	1,420	520	750	1,000	630	650
ARMAMENT	11,000 KG Bombs	1,800 KG Bombs	2,720 KG Bombs	8 AAMs	1,360 KG Bombs	4,000 KG Bombs
WINGSPAN (M)	9 (Swept)	9	12	13	9	17

remained essentially the same as those formerly performed by the Tactical Air Armies, but incorporate the introduction of more modern and capable aircraft and reflect changes in pilot training.

In addition to the increased emphasis on the achievement of air superiority in any future war, and on the importance of air power in general, the Soviets have increased their experimentation with new tactics over the last 5 years. They are developing training for a variety of new missions, including fighter escort, ECM escort, maneuvering air combat, independent search missions and air accompaniment of ground forces. They have increased the percentage of ''dissimilar'' intercept training, and the number of multi-event training sorties.

As the new training becomes more widespread, it will greatly improve Soviet capabilities to perform air missions under a variety of conditions. Many of the new missions place a much greater demand on pilot initiative and independence than was previously the case in the Soviet Air Forces. The training not only increases capabilities, it will also maximize the effective use of the new Soviet fighters, allowing Soviet pilots to take better advantage of the increased range, weapons and maneuvering capabilities of these aircraft.

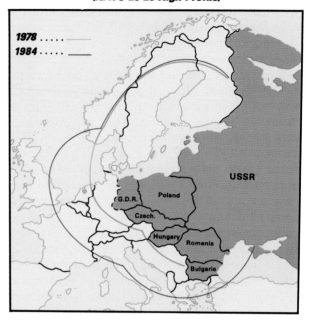

Soviet Ground Attack Aircraft (Capabilities Against NATO)

(NATO Lo-Lo-High Profile)

Their new fighter aircraft, the MiG-29/FULCRUM and the Su-27/FLANKER, are supersonic, all-weather counter-air fighters with look-down/shoot-down weapon systems and beyond-visual-range air-to-air missiles. These aircraft may have a secondary ground

Su-27/FLANKER, bottom, and MiG-29/FULCRUM aircraft.

attack role. The FULCRUM in particular may have a true dual-role capability similar to that of the US F-16 and F-18.

Soviet air forces in the Western TVD have by far the highest percentage of modern aircraft—over 90 percent of their inventory—because the Soviets perceive that this TVD faces the strongest enemy and the most dense and complicated target array. The air assets in this region number about 2,850 aircraft and include every operational Soviet airframe except the FOXHOUND. Capabilities in this area are believed to be very good and constantly improving.

US Tactical Air Forces

US tactical air forces retain a qualitative advantage over those of the Soviet Union in aircraft and weapons, and, more importantly, in personnel and training. Air combat in the Middle East demonstrated the lethality of US-built air-to-air missiles. US Air Force and Navy air crews receive about twice as much flying time as do their Soviet counterparts, and US training exercises are considered superior to those of the Soviets. Non-US NATO countries generally provide about as much flying time for their air crews as do the Soviets.

Soviet Military Power 1983 *provided initial evidence of deployment of the subsonic, close air support Su-25/FROGFOOT fighter. At left, the FROGFOOT photographed in operations over Afghanistan.*

Air support to the Southwestern TVD is generally comparable to the Western TVD. There are fewer aircraft in this area, however, because it faces a numerically smaller NATO force. Soviet air forces in this region total some 1,250 aircraft.

The Northwestern TVD has a very small number of air assets, reflecting less emphasis on air support in this region. It has few long-range aircraft; there are no FENCERs in this region, although some could be allocated from other areas. The Soviets continue to modernize their Air Forces in the Far East with late-model FLOGGER and FENCER aircraft. Currently, 1,800 aircraft, over 90 percent of which are third-generation, are in position for operations against China and Japan. The Soviets also have about 170 long- and medium-range bombers in the Far East. Of this number, some 40 BACKFIRE bombers are assigned to the Soviet Air Forces in the region.

The US and NATO Allies have also been carrying out a force modernization program over the last 5 years. The United States has recently added the A-10, the F-15 and the F-16 aircraft. The NATO Allies are also adding F-16 and TORNADO aircraft, and both the United States and NATO are adding the E-3A AWACS.

The high-performance F-14 fighter, designed for fleet air defense and air-to-air combat, is operating on more than 80 percent of the Navy's aircraft carriers with additional procurement planned. The F/A-18, which will replace the F-4 and A-7 in the Navy and Marine Corps, can accomplish both air-to-air fighter and air-to-ground attack missions. The Marine Corps' AV-8B HARRIER is scheduled to be operational by 1985, and six active light-attack squadrons will have received this new version by FY 1988. To keep pace with the anticipated threat, both the F-15 and F-16 aircraft are receiving radar modifications to enhance air-to-air target detection ranges and will also be modified to carry advanced medium range air-to-air missiles. Production of F-15s and F-16s will continue into the 1990s.

Soviet Ground Forces

Out of a total of 194 active tank, motorized rifle and airborne divisions in the Soviet force, 65 are located in the western USSR, 30 in Eastern Europe and an additional 20 in the Transcaucasus and North Caucasus Military Districts (MDs). All these divisions would likely be committed to offensive operations against NATO. In addition to these forces, 17 low-strength divisions, centrally located in the USSR, constitute the Strategic Reserves. For operation in the Southern Theater the Soviets have in place six divisions in the Turkestan MD and four engaged in combat operations in Afghanistan. These forces would be reinforced by the 20 divisions from the Caucasus MDs if they were not engaged against NATO. Soviet forces for operations in the Far East are composed of 52 tank and motorized rifle divisions. The six Warsaw Pact Allies of the Soviet Union have a total of 55 active divisions, which, collectively with Soviet divisions, amount to 249 combat divisions. Many of these divisions, most notably those in the interior of the USSR, are at low stages of readiness.

The Soviets also maintain 17 mobilization bases, predominantly in the western USSR, that could form additional combat divisions. These bases usually contain the combat equipment needed to form new divisions and would require augmentation in manpower and a substantial amount of training before they could be committed to combat operations.

While technological improvements to hardware continue throughout the Soviet force, priority is given to the forces opposite NATO, giving them the capability to conduct rapid offensive operations, characterized by shock action, massive firepower and high mobility. Surface-to-air, surface-to-surface missiles, air and air defense assets have already been discussed. Additionally, the Soviets continue to modernize and expand ground equipment such as tanks, artillery and helicopters.

Tanks: The Soviet tank force has been undergoing a major upgrade since the mid-1960s, when the first truly modern post-World War II tank, the T-64, was introduced. The first model of the T-64 was followed by at least one improved version, the T-64A, and several variants of the T-72. The most modern Soviet tank, the T-80, featuring nuclear, biological, and chemical protection and enhanced firepower and survivability, is in production; more than one thousand have been deployed to the Groups of Soviet Forces in Eastern Europe. A dramatic shift in the pro-

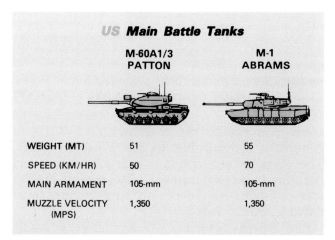

US *Main Battle Tanks*		
	M-60A1/3 PATTON	M-1 ABRAMS
WEIGHT (MT)	51	55
SPEED (KM/HR)	50	70
MAIN ARMAMENT	105-mm	105-mm
MUZZLE VELOCITY (MPS)	1,350	1,350

USSR *Main Battle Tanks*					
	T-54/55	T-62	T-64	T-72	T-80
WEIGHT (MT)	36	37	35	41	42
SPEED (KM/HR)	50	50	50	60	60
MAIN ARMAMENT	100-mm	115-mm	125-mm	125-mm	125-mm
MUZZLE VELOCITY (MPS)	1,400	1,600	1,750	1,750	1,750

portion of these modern tanks, as part of the total Soviet inventory opposite NATO, has occurred. The impact on the most critical area—the one opposite the NATO center—is particularly significant. In this area, T-64, T-72, T-80 tanks comprise about 50 percent of the total. Over 1,400 T-80 tanks have been deployed opposite NATO.

The T-80 main battle tank is now in its third year of production.

Artillery: The Soviets are pursuing a comprehensive program of upgrading and expanding the artillery fire support available to ground forces. Several new artillery pieces, some of which are nuclear-capable, and new multiple rocket launchers have been introduced in the past few years. Simultaneously, an ongoing divisional reorganization has result-

ed in increases in the towed and self-propelled artillery assets. The addition of an artillery battalion to tank regiments is intended to make tank and motorized rifle divisions fully capable combined arms forces.

122-mm self-propelled howitzer

Several developments illustrate Soviet technological improvements to the artillery force. Two new 152-mm guns, one self-propelled and one towed, have been fielded since 1978, and both are deployed with Soviet forces in Eastern Europe. They are nuclear-capable and replace pieces that were not.

As an additional complement to surface-to-surface missiles, the Soviets are continuing deployment of nuclear-capable heavy artillery brigades armed with mobile 240-mm self-propelled mortars and the 203-mm self-propelled guns. Deployment of the 203-mm gun outside the USSR in 1982, coupled with the appearance of the new 152-mm guns in the same year, indicates the importance Soviet doctrine places on capability to deliver low-yield nuclear strikes relatively close to Soviet forces.

A 220-mm multiple rocket launcher has been deployed opposite NATO since 1978. Each mobile launcher has 16 tubes and can fire chemical as well as conventional high explosive munitions.

Helicopters: Soviet helicopter forces are receiving priority attention with continuing upgrades in numbers, units and technology. Divisional helicopter assets continue to increase in number and, overall, the rotary wing force continues to figure prominently in Soviet doctrine and tactics. All major training exercises routinely feature large numbers of helicopters integrated into all facets of com-

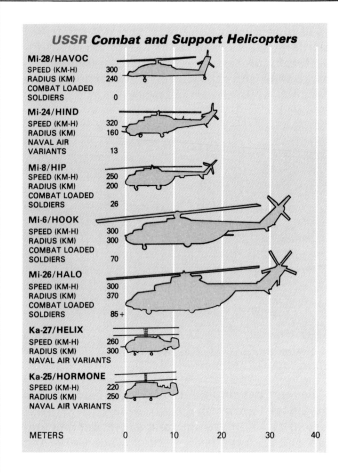

USSR Combat and Support Helicopters

Mi-28/HAVOC
SPEED (KM-H)	300
RADIUS (KM)	240
COMBAT LOADED SOLDIERS	0

Mi-24/HIND
SPEED (KM-H)	320
RADIUS (KM)	160
NAVAL AIR VARIANTS	13

Mi-8/HIP
SPEED (KM-H)	250
RADIUS (KM)	200
COMBAT LOADED SOLDIERS	26

Mi-6/HOOK
SPEED (KM-H)	300
RADIUS (KM)	300
COMBAT LOADED SOLDIERS	70

Mi-26/HALO
SPEED (KM-H)	300
RADIUS (KM)	370
COMBAT LOADED SOLDIERS	85 +

Ka-27/HELIX
SPEED (KM-H)	260
RADIUS (KM)	300
NAVAL AIR VARIANTS	

Ka-25/HORMONE
SPEED (KM-H)	220
RADIUS (KM)	250
NAVAL AIR VARIANTS	

METERS   0   10   20   30   40

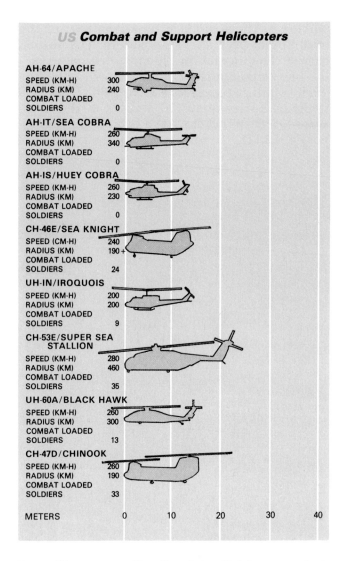

US Combat and Support Helicopters

AH-64/APACHE
SPEED (KM-H)	300
RADIUS (KM)	240
COMBAT LOADED SOLDIERS	0

AH-IT/SEA COBRA
SPEED (KM-H)	260
RADIUS (KM)	340
COMBAT LOADED SOLDIERS	0

AH-IS/HUEY COBRA
SPEED (KM-H)	260
RADIUS (KM)	230
COMBAT LOADED SOLDIERS	0

CH-46E/SEA KNIGHT
SPEED (CM-H)	240
RADIUS (KM)	190 +
COMBAT LOADED SOLDIERS	24

UH-IN/IROQUOIS
SPEED (KM-H)	200
RADIUS (KM)	200
COMBAT LOADED SOLDIERS	9

CH-53E/SUPER SEA STALLION
SPEED (KM-H)	280
RADIUS (KM)	460
COMBAT LOADED SOLDIERS	35

UH-60A/BLACK HAWK
SPEED (KM-H)	260
RADIUS (KM)	300
COMBAT LOADED SOLDIERS	13

CH-47D/CHINOOK
SPEED (KM-H)	260
RADIUS (KM)	190
COMBAT LOADED SOLDIERS	33

METERS   0   10   20   30   40

bined arms operations. Soviet helicopter forces continue to lead new advances in doctrinal developments, such as airmobile assault forces, and provide major support to other forces, such as the Operational Maneuver Groups. Tactically, they continue to provide significant combat power to Soviet forces operating in Afghanistan.

Soviet combat helicopters are among the most heavily armed in the world — the Mi-24/HIND E and Mi-8/HIP E attack helicopters and the Mi-8/HIP C and Mi-17/HIP H assault helicopters offer Soviet commanders a considerable degree of flexibility in the application of intense firepower. The Soviets are testing operational concepts in Afganistan, modifying tactics as the war proceeds. These lessons, while not directly applicable to a European war, would add to Soviet effectiveness in general conflict.

The Soviets continue to develop new systems designed to take advantage of increasingly sophisticated technology. New, more agile, powerful helicopters, such as the HAVOC, with improved armament and significantly improved performance and survivabil-

ity will ensure the Soviets field a combat effective helicopter force in the late 1980s and early 1990s.

US Ground Forces

US military strategy does not call for matching the size of the Soviet ground forces, but instead emphasizes refining the US qualitative edge in conjunction with moderate force increases.

The US Army and Marine Corps are developing organizational changes to improve combat effectiveness. The Army is undertaking a program entitled "Army 90" to implement its Air Land Battle doctrine. This doctrine has been developed to synchronize the close-in battle against enemy lead forces with a longer-range battle against enemy follow-on forces. Army light and heavy divisions are being rearmed and restructured for sustained, continuous combat operations at any level of conflict. The Army is seeking to increase the strategic mobility of its light divisions while capitalizing on systems to increase overall firepower and combat effectiveness.

The Marine Corps is restructuring infantry battalions to increase firepower and tactical mobility. Introduction of more advanced weapons will improve combat capabilities. A 25-percent increase in DRAGON antitank missile teams in each battalion and an additional TOW antitank missile platoon in each regiment will improve antiarmor capabilities.

The present generation of antiarmor weapons includes the long-range TOW, medium-range DRAGON and light antitank short-range missiles. Improved warheads and guidance systems will increase the TOW's ability to penetrate new Soviet armor.

By the end of the decade, the Army is scheduled to have over 1,500 attack helicopters, two-thirds of which will be the AH-1 COBRA TOW. The Army's AH-64 APACHE helicopter, which entered production in 1982, is an advanced, quick-reaction, antitank weapon. It is armed with 16 HELLFIRE antiarmor missiles, a 30-mm automatic gun, and 2.75 inch rockets.

The M1 ABRAMS main battle tank has been deployed in Army field units since 1981. The M1 provides US forces with improved mobility, survivability and antiarmor firepower. The Army plans to replace the M1 main gun with the German-designed 120-mm main gun system, which would be interoperable with the German LEOPARD II tank gun.

The Multiple-Launch Rocket System (MLRS), a cooperative program with the Federal Republic of Germany, France, Italy and the United Kingdom, was fielded with US forces in 1983. It is designed to give NATO ground forces enhanced firepower to suppress enemy artillery and introduces a new capability to interdict enemy operations beyond normal artillery range.

The BRADLEY Fighting Vehicle, introduced in 1981, is modernizing Army mechanized forces. These vehicles are armed with 25-mm automatic cannons, 7.62-mm coaxial machine guns, and TOW antitank weapons. They give mechanized infantry a true mounted combat capability. Introduction of a new Light Armored Vehicle will provide the Marine Corps units with increased mobility and firepower.

Soviet Naval Forces

The Soviet Navy maintains a world naval presence. The Navy is composed of four fleets—Northern, Baltic, Black, and Pacific—and the Caspian Sea Flotilla. Each of the four fleets has submarine, surface, air, naval infantry (marines) and coastal defense components as well as large ashore support, training and administrative organizations. In all, there are over 467,000 personnel in the Soviet Navy, about 186,000 of whom are aboard ship.

The years 1967-1968 were watershed years for the Soviet Navy; the Soviets introduced lead units of their second generation missile-equipped submarines and surface ships. It was also the period when they began in earn-

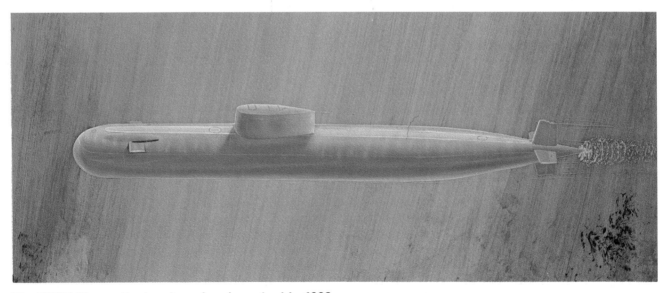

The MIKE-Class attack submarine, launched in 1983.

61   Chapter III Theater Forces

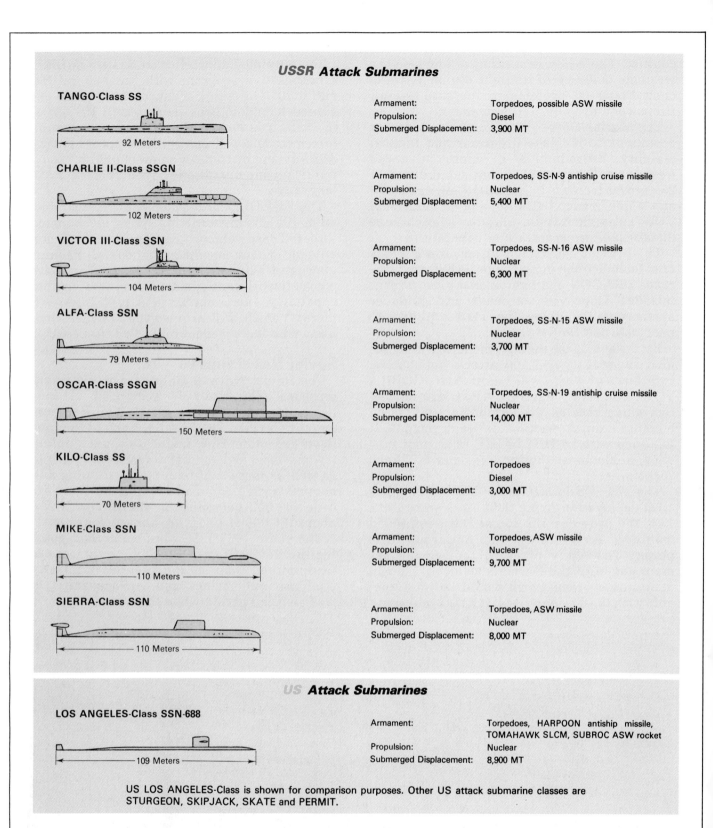

USSR Attack Submarines

TANGO-Class SS
92 Meters

Armament:	Torpedoes, possible ASW missile
Propulsion:	Diesel
Submerged Displacement:	3,900 MT

CHARLIE II-Class SSGN
102 Meters

Armament:	Torpedoes, SS-N-9 antiship cruise missile
Propulsion:	Nuclear
Submerged Displacement:	5,400 MT

VICTOR III-Class SSN
104 Meters

Armament:	Torpedoes, SS-N-16 ASW missile
Propulsion:	Nuclear
Submerged Displacement:	6,300 MT

ALFA-Class SSN
79 Meters

Armament:	Torpedoes, SS-N-15 ASW missile
Propulsion:	Nuclear
Submerged Displacement:	3,700 MT

OSCAR-Class SSGN
150 Meters

Armament:	Torpedoes, SS-N-19 antiship cruise missile
Propulsion:	Nuclear
Submerged Displacement:	14,000 MT

KILO-Class SS
70 Meters

Armament:	Torpedoes
Propulsion:	Diesel
Submerged Displacement:	3,000 MT

MIKE-Class SSN
110 Meters

Armament:	Torpedoes, ASW missile
Propulsion:	Nuclear
Submerged Displacement:	9,700 MT

SIERRA-Class SSN
110 Meters

Armament:	Torpedoes, ASW missile
Propulsion:	Nuclear
Submerged Displacement:	8,000 MT

US Attack Submarines

LOS ANGELES-Class SSN-688
109 Meters

Armament:	Torpedoes, HARPOON antiship missile, TOMAHAWK SLCM, SUBROC ASW rocket
Propulsion:	Nuclear
Submerged Displacement:	8,900 MT

US LOS ANGELES-Class is shown for comparison purposes. Other US attack submarine classes are STURGEON, SKIPJACK, SKATE and PERMIT.

est to deploy combat forces away from home waters. Since then, the Soviet Navy has developed into a globally deployed force composed of an impressive array of ships, submarines and aircraft, includng the nuclear-powered guided missile cruiser KIROV.

In the past year, there have been significant developments in ship construction programs and deployment activities. In the construction area, two new classes of nuclear-powered attack submarines were launched—MIKE and SIERRA. Two other classes—the nuclear-powered high-speed ALFA-Class and the diesel-powered TANGO—may have completed their production runs and their follow-on classes are expected to appear soon. The Soviets have begun construction of a large aircraft carrier, with an estimated displacement of some 60,000 tons.

The newer submarine classes introduced in the 1980s, as well as the 1979 VICTOR III SSN, have improved technologies and capabilities. They are generally larger in size and have a greater weapons capacity. Prior to 1978, the Soviets emphasized the construction of ballistic missile submarines. Since then, however, production emphasis has shifted, and about 75 percent are now torpedo or cruise missile attack submarines. During the next 10 years, while there may be a slight decline in the total number of attack submarines, there will be a significant growth in the number of nuclear-powered units.

The MIKE-Class, at over 9,700 tons displacement, and the SIERRA-Class, at about 8,000 tons, are indicative of the trend toward increasing the size of Soviet submarines. The SIERRA is about 20 percent larger than its immediate predecessor, the VICTOR III, which was introduced only 4 years earlier.

The Soviets are continuing to build high technology submarines that have pressure hulls made of titanium. This development enables Soviet submarines to operate at great depths in addition to being more survivable as a result of greater hull strength.

Important force developments also have included the activation of the second unit of the OSCAR-Class nuclear-powered cruise missile submarine; the beginning of sea trials of the

HOTEL II-Class SSBNs carry three SS-N-5 SLBMs and eight torpedoes.

63

The SLAVA-Class guided missile cruiser.

second KIROV-Class nuclear-powered guided missile cruiser; the addition of five other attack submarines; six major surface combatants; 46 fighter-bombers; over 40 helicopters, mostly ASW versions; and one long-range ASW BEAR F. Late in 1983, the third unit of the KIEV-Class carriers and the second unit of the IVAN ROGOV-Class amphibious assault ships departed for the Pacific Fleet via the Indian Ocean. Earlier, the SLAVA-Class

cruiser—provisionally identified last year as the KRASINA-Class—made her maiden voyage out of area from the Black Sea to the Northern Fleet and back again.

The aircraft carrier being built at Nikolayev on the Black Sea is assessed to be nuclear powered, and it is expected to have a full-length flight deck. Because it is likely that this ship is being designed to carry conventional take off and landing aircraft, instead of

the KIEV's vertical take off and landing type, it will probably be fitted with arresting gear and steam catapults like those on US aircraft carriers. This ship and her new aircraft will begin tests before the end of the decade.

The new class of Soviet carriers will help to eliminate deficiencies in two areas. The first is air defense of their naval forces beyond the ranges of land-based fighter aircraft. Secondly, the Soviets have an active interest in improving their distant area power projection capabilities to become more influential in the Third World. To achieve this goal, they need to be able to provide air protection for naval forces as well as to protect and assist ground forces operating ashore. Thus, it is expected that the aircraft on the new carrier will have both air-to-air and ground support mission capabilities.

At Cam Ranh Bay, Vietnam and in the Dahlak Archipelago off Ethiopia in the southern Red Sea, the Soviets have achieved signifi-

Chapter III Theater Forces

cant gains in access to important naval support facilities. The most critical operational developments have taken place at Cam Ranh Bay where the Soviets have upgraded and increased the size of their forces. In 1982, the Soviets had about 15 warships and auxiliaries operating in the South China Sea. Since early 1983, the number has ranged from 20 to 25 ships. Naval long-range BEAR D reconnaissance and BEAR F antisubmarine warfare (ASW) aircraft continue to operate in the area. In late 1983, the Soviets began to augment this capability, and thus far, about 10 strike, tanker, and electronic combat variants of the medium-range Tu-16 BADGER have deployed to Cam Ranh Bay.

During the past year, the Soviets have become more heavily entrenched at Dahlak. The Soviet Navy apparently has now achieved exclusive use of the island, and Ethiopian nationals rarely visit. In addition, the Soviets have begun to improve the island's defenses with antiaircraft weapons and a contingent of their naval infantry.

Remote facilities provide the Soviets immediate access to the vital sea lanes that link the natural resources of these regions to the industries of the United States and its Allies.

In the fall of 1983, the Soviets conducted their first world-wide naval exercise since 1975. The exercise was unique in at least two respects. First, while the exercise did em-

KARA-Class guided missile cruisers were the first to carry three separate missile systems.

phasize traditional homeland protection, with anticarrier and antisubmarine activities, there was also a focus on anti-sea lines of communication and convoy operations in ocean areas including the South China Sea and the Indian Ocean. The Soviets even augmented their Indian Ocean deployed submarine forces with units that had been operating off Vietnam. The exercise clearly demonstrated the military availability of Soviet civilian maritime assets, when a large number of merchant and fishing fleet ships were integrated into naval operations, either as part of convoys or simulating enemy forces.

The Soviet Navy has continued to focus developmental efforts on incorporating increasing levels of advanced technology and sophistication into all their ships. They continue to build even larger ships with equally heightened levels of lethality in their weapons systems and greater endurance to facilitate deployments to all seas and oceans.

US Naval Forces

Measured by numbers of ships, the United States and its Allies maintain a favorable balance of maritime power. The United States and its NATO Allies maintain about 1,500 ships, compared to a Warsaw Pact force of about 1,400. The United States and its Allies hold a significant lead in ships of over 1,000 tons displacement.

This aggregate comparison reflects several areas of Western advantage. For example, the West has an advantage in carrier air power, an advantage expected to grow during the 1980s as the United States builds its force from the current level of 13 carriers to 15 by the end of the decade. Upgrading and recommissioning of the battleship NEW JERSEY and sister ships of the IOWA-Class are adding significant firepower to the US fleet. The United States maintains a superior amphibious assault force, with about four times the tonnage of its Soviet counterpart. The United States and its Allies also have an important advantage in underway replenishment ships and other naval support forces, enabling Western forces to operate in distant waters with more endurance and self sufficiency.

Qualitatively, Western maritime forces have an important edge in antisubmarine warfare. Today, the United States also maintains qualitative superiority in its submarine forces, especially in sound quieting and detection capabilities.

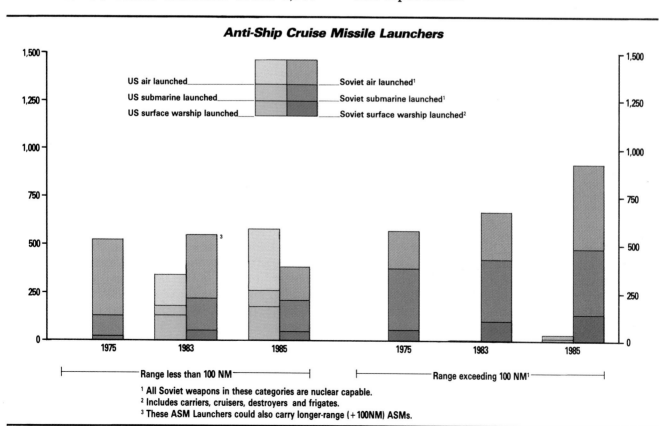

Anti-Ship Cruise Missile Launchers

US air launched — Soviet air launched[1]
US submarine launched — Soviet submarine launched[1]
US surface warship launched — Soviet surface warship launched[2]

Range less than 100 NM   Range exceeding 100 NM[1]

[1] All Soviet weapons in these categories are nuclear capable.
[2] Includes carriers, cruisers, destroyers and frigates.
[3] These ASM Launchers could also carry longer-range (+100NM) ASMs.

Chapter III Theater Forces

Surface Ship Comparisons

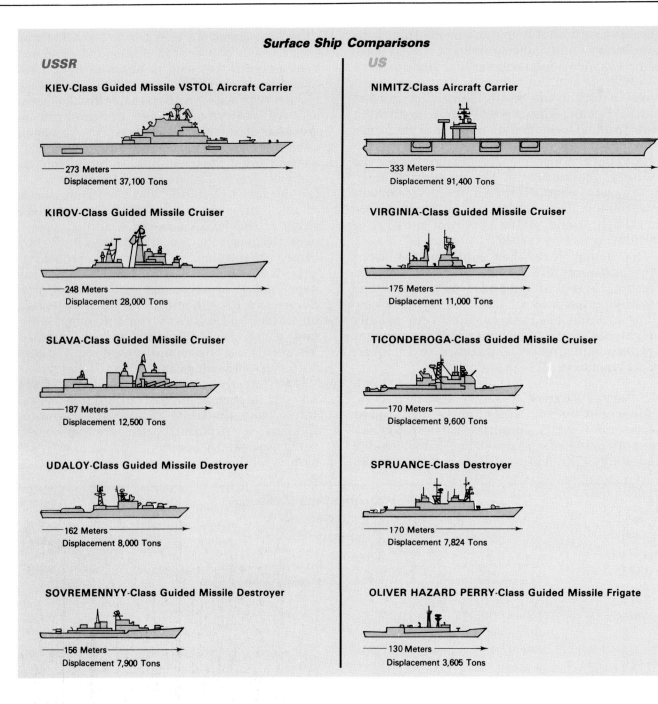

USSR

KIEV-Class Guided Missile VSTOL Aircraft Carrier
273 Meters
Displacement 37,100 Tons

KIROV-Class Guided Missile Cruiser
248 Meters
Displacement 28,000 Tons

SLAVA-Class Guided Missile Cruiser
187 Meters
Displacement 12,500 Tons

UDALOY-Class Guided Missile Destroyer
162 Meters
Displacement 8,000 Tons

SOVREMENNYY-Class Guided Missile Destroyer
156 Meters
Displacement 7,900 Tons

US

NIMITZ-Class Aircraft Carrier
333 Meters
Displacement 91,400 Tons

VIRGINIA-Class Guided Missile Cruiser
175 Meters
Displacement 11,000 Tons

TICONDEROGA-Class Guided Missile Cruiser
170 Meters
Displacement 9,600 Tons

SPRUANCE-Class Destroyer
170 Meters
Displacement 7,824 Tons

OLIVER HAZARD PERRY-Class Guided Missile Frigate
130 Meters
Displacement 3,605 Tons

The Soviet Navy has been a leader for many years in the development and deployment of naval antiship cruise missiles. The United States is now upgrading its own units through large-scale deployments of HARPOON and TOMAHAWK cruise missiles.

The United States and its Allies are pursuing several programs designed to strengthen NATO collective maritime defense capabilities. To improve antisubmarine warfare forces, the United States is continuing construction of the highly capable LOS ANGE-

LES-Class attack submarine, with production rates gradually being accelerated. The delivery of 34 new FFG-7 frigates since 1977 has added significantly to the ASW capabilities of US surface forces. New towed-array sonar systems now being deployed aboard increasing numbers of US surface warships, coupled with the ongoing introduction of new LAMPS MK III helicopters, will also substantially enhance the long-range ASW attack capabilities of US surface combatants. The United States is also modernizing its force of land-based, long-range P-3 maritime patrol aircraft in order to improve the capability to locate and destroy enemy submarines in forward areas and barriers before they come within range of Allied naval forces and convoys. Improved torpedoes and ASW rockets now in production or under development will provide improvements needed to counter Soviet submarines that are faster, dive deeper, and have reduced acoustic target strength.

The United States is steadily improving its capability for anti-air warfare with construction of additional CG-47 Aegis guided missile cruisers and planned introduction of a new class of guided missile destroyers in the latter half of the decade. In addition, significant modernization is ongoing for existing guided missile cruisers and current carrier based AEW aircraft and is planned for the F-14 force. Finally, strong self-air-defense capabilities are being provided to all maritime forces, commensurate with the threat they could face.

Special Purpose Forces (SPETSNAZ)

The USSR maintains a complement of special purpose forces, known by the Soviet acronym SPETSNAZ. These special purpose forces are controlled by the Main Intelligence Directorate (GRU) of the Soviet General Staff and are trained to conduct a variety of sensitive missions, including covert action abroad. This latter mission was illustrated by their covert role, under KGB direction, in the December 1979 assassination of Afghan President Hafizullah Amin, which was performed by a joint KGB/SPETSNAZ force.

During peacetime, the GRU carefully coordinates reconnaissance programs that are geared to meet the intelligence requirements for Soviet forces in war. In wartime, SPETSNAZ forces would operate far behind enemy lines for extended periods of time. They would conduct sabotage, reconnaissance and attacks on a wide variety of military and political targets.

The KGB is assessed to have responsibility, under Central Committee guidance, for operational planning, coordination and political control of special purpose forces that operate abroad in peacetime. This was the case in the Soviet invasion of Czechoslovakia in 1968, and of Afghanistan in 1979. The KGB maintains its own special operations capabilities in the form of clandestine assets dedicated to assassination and wartime sabotage.

Wartime missions of GRU special purpose troops are planned under the direction of the General Staff and are integral to the Soviet combined arms operations. Intended to support theater as well as front or fleet-level operations, SPETSNAZ forces are capable of operating throughout the enemy homeland.

SPETSNAZ would be employed to attack NATO forces in wartime. Training facilities for these Special Purpose Forces feature mock-ups of Western weapons systems.

Organized into brigades, these forces will infiltrate and fight as small teams. In a war, each of these brigades can be expected to field approximately 100 SPETSNAZ teams. A typical team would be composed of an officer as leader with a warrant officer or senior sergeant as second in command. Other members of the group are trained as radio operators and weapons and demolition experts. In addition to the normal military training, all are trained in:
- infiltration tactics,
- sabotage methods using explosives, incendiaries, acids, and abrasives,
- parachute training,
- clandestine communications,

- hand-to-hand combat and silent killing techniques.
- language/customs of target country.
- survival behind enemy lines and
- reconnaissance and target location.

To make training as realistic as possible, SPETSNAZ brigades have facilities equipped with accurate full-scale models of key targets such as enemy installations and weapon systems. The brigades intended for operations against NATO share similar demolition training and equipment familiarization. Training facilities are equipped with mockups of NATO nuclear systems including Pershing, Lance, and GLCM, as well as airfields, nuclear storage sites, and communications facilities. The missions of SPETSNAZ make a significant addition to Soviet combat forces.

In both peace and war, these SPETSNAZ forces represent an important threat. In peacetime, they are a formidable instrument with which the Soviets can project limited, but decisive, force abroad, especially into the Third World. In war, major facilities and important weapons systems are the object of their attacks.

US Special Operations Forces

US special operations forces are valuable elements available to field commanders. The potential benefits of such forces justify the high priority given to the revitalization of their capabilities. Special operations forces are particularly well qualified to counter threats to US interests that result from low-intensity conflict. In this regard, special operations forces have accounted for one-quarter of the mobile training teams deployed in support of US security assistance programs since 1979.

Special operations forces are also capable of direct action in response to crises for which the use of other US forces might be inappropriate. Such crises might include threats of hostile acts against US citizens or facilities abroad by terrorists, dissidents, foreign governments or other sources. Special operations forces are especially useful in resolving crises and terminating conflicts that are still at relatively low levels of violence and to which the nations involved have not made major resource commitments.

Special operations forces must also be capable of supporting conventional forces in the event of large-scale Soviet aggression against the United States and its Allies. To this end, special operations forces can provide invaluable intelligence to conventional field commanders and may conduct psychological, civil affairs and unconventional warfare operations. Unconventional warfare missions would include the interrelated fields of guerrilla warfare, direct action and evasion and escape operations.

Accelerated action is under way to improve special operations capabilities to meet national and theater requirements in peace, crisis and war.

Soviet Chemical Warfare

The Soviet Union has the world's largest, best equipped and best trained military force for waging chemical warfare. The extensive modernization and growth of the Armed Forces include a dynamic and viable program to strengthen the USSR's chemical warfare capabilities.

The Soviet Union continues to test, produce and stockpile chemical weapons. Moreover, the Soviets have developed the doctrine, plans, personnel and equipment to support their use of chemical weapons. They believe that the user of chemical weapons would gain a significant military advantage in a conventional conflict. Their continued testing of chemical weapons, the enlarged storage capacity of chemical agents and weapons and the existence of active production facilities are among the indicators of a serious chemical weapons program. These indications and strong evidence of the actual use of chemical and toxin weapons by the Soviet Union and its client forces in Afghanistan, Laos and Kampuchea reflect their drive to strengthen and improve their capability to wage chemical warfare and their willingness to employ such weapons in battlefield situations.

Soviet research and development of militarily useful chemical warfare agents covers a wide range of applications. New chemical agents and combinations of agents, including ways to render the protective masks and filtration systems of potential enemies ineffective, are being investigated. One group of agents, known as mycotoxins, has been identified in the laboratory from samples collected in Afghanistan.

Almost all Soviet conventional land, sea and air weapon systems, from mortars to long-range tactical missiles, are capable of firing chemical ammunition or warheads. The Soviets have developed the data required to use these chemical weapons in battle situations, which includes the types and numbers of weapons required to attack various targets under a variety of weather and combat conditions. Currently they are exploring and testing systems with larger payload, increased range, and better accuracy for greater target flexibility and a deeper strike capability. They have developed two types of chemical weapons for their tactical missiles, bulk agents for a single large warhead and bomblets that can be dispersed over the target.

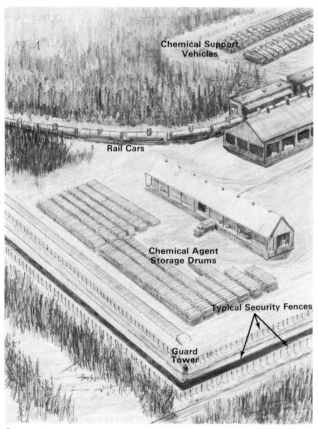

Chemical Depot

In accordance with their doctrine, once release authority has been granted for employment of chemical weapons, the appropriate commander may be ordered to conduct strikes against any or all identified targets. He may use persistent agents or non-persistent agents as well as a variety of delivery systems, and will know the level of contamination to place on the target. Should his own forces have to cross a contaminated area, the filtration system on all combat vehicles will help allow his

troops to continue to maneuver and fight, and he will have specially trained troops available for consultation, reconnaissance and decontamination.

Chemical/biological decontamination of a SCUD-B tactical missile during a Soviet field-training exercise. The Soviets have protective measures built into their ground force armored vehicles and troops trained to cleanse the outside surfaces following chemical/biological operations.

The Shikhany Chemical Warfare Proving Ground is one of the primary Soviet chemical weapons test areas. Since the late 1920s, it has grown in size and sophistication and today is an expanding and highly active chemical weapons testing facility. Since the late 1970s, the Soviets have constructed several new chemical weapon test facilities and further construction continues. At these facilities, sampling devices used to determine the efficiency of chemical weapons are arranged in grids that have a circular or rectangular pattern. These distinctive grids measure the agent concentration and how well it was dispersed. The shape of the grid and complexity of its pattern depend on the kind of weapon— bomb, artillery or rocket—and the type of agent being tested.

Chemical agents produced over the past five decades believed to be are stored in a network of military depots located across the Soviet Union. These depots are believed to contain agents in bulk containers and agent-filled munitions, as well as gas masks, protective suits, decontamination solutions and decontamination vehicles. The depots are highly secure military installations, and many have rail lines allowing for the rapid mobilization of chemical warfare materials. The amount of agents, weapons and material in storage at these depots has increased significantly since the late 1960s.

Soviet Chemical Weapons Depots

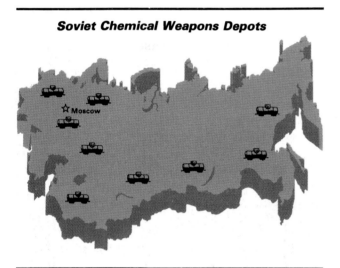

The Soviets have more than 80,000 officers and enlisted specialists trained in chemical warfare, a force that will double in wartime. They have about 30,000 special vehicles for reconnaissance and decontamination. The Soviets have established chemical military academies and more than 200 sites for teaching and training Soviet troops on how to protect and decontaminate themselves following combat. The chemical troops are responsible for the development, testing and evaluation of new chemical agents, weapon systems, antidotes, suits, gas masks, protective and decontaminating systems. In addition, they are responsible for the production and storage of chemical weapons and also serve as advisers to commanders for chemical weapons and the tactics for their use.

US Chemical Weapons
The United States is actively working in the multilateral Conference on Disarmament for a complete and verifiable ban on the development, production, stockpiling, possession, transfer and use of chemical weapons. Even in the absence of such a ban, the United States will never initiate the use of chemical weapons in a conflict. But we must maintain a credible deterrent against chemical attack that includes both protective and retaliatory capabilities. To do so, we must redress the severe imbalances that have developed as a consequence of long-term US restraint and continued Soviet expansion and modernization in the chemical weapons area.

The United States has not produced any chemical weapons for 15 years, and most of our chemical munitions could no longer be delivered effectively on the battlefield. The most critical deficiency is the lack of a capability to target enemy forces effectively with chemical agents beyond artillery range. Further, our chemical weapon and agent production facilities have deteriorated and are unusable without extensive renovation or replacement.

To have an effective deterrent, the United States need not, and will not attempt to, match the Soviets in quantities and types of chemical weapons. Instead, our aim is to have the smallest, safest stockpile that would convince the USSR it could gain no significant military advantage from the use of chemical weapons against us or our Allies. Even with their formidable protective capabilities, Soviet forces would face severe difficulties in sustaining combat operations if they faced counterattack with chemicals. We are improving the utility of our current stockpile through maintenance, planning and training. However, these activities cannot redress the most critical stockpile deficiencies, and, thus, we are also seeking to reestablish a capability to produce chemical weapons, and to overcome these critical stockpile deficiencies by acquiring an effective deep-strike chemical weapon and a modern artillery projectile.

In addition, US forces must be able to defend against chemical attack. We have recently made considerable progress in this regard. Chemical-related training has increased in all services. Individual protective equipment is available to Army, Air Force and Marine units, and the Navy is in the process of equipping its personnel. Additionally, new ship construction programs will include degrees of collective protective systems to improve staying power in a chemical warfare environment. We have also fielded improved detection equipment. Nevertheless, US chemical protective capability still needs improvement in such areas as protective clothing, collective protection systems, detection, warning and monitoring devices, decontamination equipment and agents and the ability to treat casualties in a chemical warfare environment. We have research and development programs in all these areas. Despite the necessity for improved defenses against chemical attack, we must also recognize that the effectiveness of troops is significantly diminished if they are required to operate in a chemical protective posture. Deterrence of chemical attack remains essential.

Soviet Biological Warfare

The Soviet Union has an active R&D program to investigate and evaluate the utility of biological weapons and their impact on the combat environment. The Soviet effort in biological warfare violates the Biological and Toxin Weapons Convention of 1972, which was ratified by the USSR. The convention bans the research, development, production and possession of biological agents and toxins for warfare purposes.

There are at least seven biological warfare centers in the USSR that have the highest security and are under the strictest military control. One of these is located in the city of Sverdlovsk. In the spring of 1979, an accidental release of an anthrax agent occurred there, either as a result of a leakage in a containment system or an explosion. A large quantity of anthrax traveled at least four kilometers downwind from the facility and caused a significant number of casualties and deaths. More than 3,000 Soviet citizens may have been infected. As a result of the accident, large sections of Sverdlovsk were placed under quarantine and military control. Strenuous efforts were made by Soviet doctors to treat victims, and a large-scale effort to decontaminate the area was undertaken. The Soviet Government has claimed that the anthrax problem was caused by the illegal sale of contaminated meat on the black market. The evidence indicates instead that the victims suffered from pulmonary anthrax caused by the inhalation of an anthrax agent, which could only have escaped from the military facility.

Soviet research efforts in the area of genetic engineering may also have a connection with their biological warfare program. There is an

apparent effort on the part of the Soviets to transfer selected aspects of genetic engineering research to their biological warfare centers. For biological warfare purposes, genetic engineering could open a large number of possibilities. Normally harmless, non-disease producing organisms could be modified to become highly toxic or produce diseases for which an opponent has no known treatment or cure. Other agents, now considered too unstable for storage or biological warfare applications, could be changed sufficiently to be an effective agent.

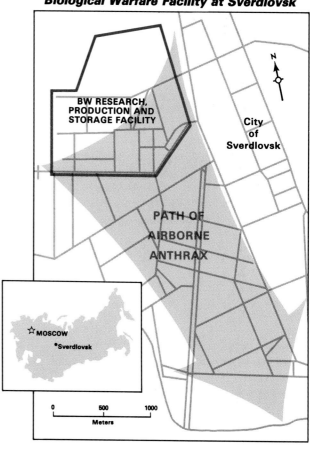

Accidental Release of Anthrax from Biological Warfare Facility at Sverdlovsk

In Soviet doctrine, the biological weapon is seen as a strategic weapon for the spread of infectious disease. Many of the Soviet long- and intermediate-range missile systems are technically capable of disseminating large quantities of disease agents over large areas.

The United States, in contrast, not only ratified the Biological and Toxic Weapons Convention of 1972, but also continues to adhere fully to that ban.

NATO and the Warsaw Pact

In May 1982, the North Atlantic Treaty Organization published the *NATO and the Warsaw Pact—Force Comparisons* study, which included the following statement in its Foreword: "The numerical balance of forces has moved slowly but steadily in favour of the Warsaw Pact over the past two decades. During this period the members of the North Atlantic Alliance have lost much of the technological advantage which permitted NATO to rely on the view that quality could compensate for quantity. It is clear that the trend is dangerous. Nevertheless the overall deterrent continues to safeguard peace."

Charts from the 1982 NATO study were published in *Soviet Military Power 1983*. The North Atlantic Alliance presently is preparing an updated force comparisons study. The following charts and tables, present an interim estimate of updated 1983 data.

France and Spain are members of the North Atlantic Alliance but do not participate in its integrated military structure. In an invasion of Western Europe by the Warsaw Pact, France and Spain would defend their national sovereignty with the following forces: approximately 20 divisions, 2,000 tanks, 3,000 artillery/mortars, 1,000 anti-tank launchers, 8,000 combat vehicles, 450 helicopters, 900 aircraft and 200 naval ships and craft.

The chart at right shows those forces in place in Europe. If US early reinforcements are added to each category, the NATO-Warsaw Pact ground force comparison would be as shown in the following table:

NATO/Warsaw Pact Force Comparison

	NATO	Warsaw Pact
Divisions	93	176
Tanks	14,400	42,600
Anti-Tank	15,300	32,200
Artillery	11,500	35,000
Combat Vehicles	35,700	75,000
Attack Helicopters	775	960

NATO/Warsaw Pact Combat Aircraft in Place in Europe[1]

	Fighter-Bomber Ground-Attack	Interceptor[2]	Reconnaissance	Bombers
NATO	1,975	780	235	—
Warsaw Pact	2,250	4,195	585	400

NOTE: US reinforcing aircraft are: 1,300; 225; 173; 62 respectively.
[1] Excludes France and Spain.
[2] Many interceptors can be used in ground-attack roles.

NATO Naval Forces

	1971	1981	1983[1]
Aircraft carriers	9	7	13
Helicopter carriers	6	2	0
Cruisers	11	15	23
Destroyers/frigates	381	274	296
Coastal escorts and fast patrol boats	180	167	192
Amphibious ships			
Ocean-going	24	41	71
Independent coastal craft	62	69	69
Mine warfare ships	349	257	273
Total submarines	195	190	197
Ballistic missile submarines	38[2]	35[2]	35
Long-range attack submarines	72	60	120
Other types	85	95	42
% NATO submarines nuclear powered	50%	49%	48%
Sea-based, tactical and support aircraft (including helicopters)	801	712	949
Land-based tactical and support aircraft	112	180	325
Land-based anti-submarine warfare fixed-wing aircraft and helicopters	471	450	486

[1] Allied naval forces allocated to NATO. Excludes France and Spain.
[2] Also referred to in the section on Nuclear Forces.

Warsaw Pact Naval Forces[1]

	1971	1981	1983
KIEV-Class ships	0	2	2
Helicopter carriers	2	2	2
Cruisers	20	21	23
Destroyers, frigates and corvettes	142	179	187
Coastal escorts and patrol boats	553	551	515
Amphibious ships			
Ocean-going ships	7	16	19
Independent coastal ships and craft	190	163	176
Mine warfare ships and craft	374	354	375
Total submarines (all types)	248	258	246
Ballistic missile submarines	38[2]	52[2]	49[2]
Long-range attack and cruise missile submarines	102	144	142
Other types	108	62	55
% Submarines nuclear powered	25%	44%	49%
Sea-based, tactical and support aircraft including helicopters	36	146	181
Land-based tactical and support aircraft (including some transport aircraft and transport helicopters)	521[3]	719[3]	700[3]
Land-based anti-submarine warfare fixed-wing aircraft and helicopters	225	179	228

[1] Excluding the Pacific Fleet.
[2] Also referred to in the section on Nuclear Forces.
[3] About 300 of these are bombers.

NATO-WARSAW PACT Ground Force Comparison (In place in Europe — 1983)[1]

NATO Countries ____

WARSAW PACT Countries ____

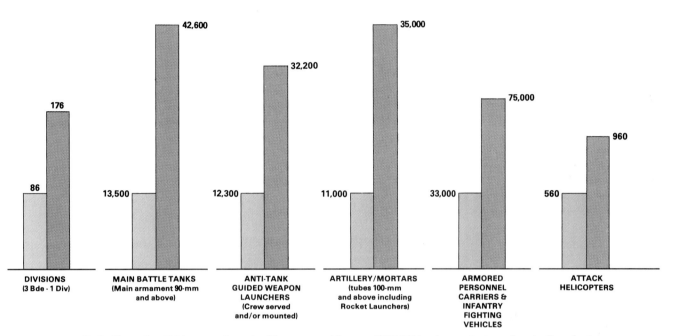

DIVISIONS (3 Bde - 1 Div)	MAIN BATTLE TANKS (Main armament 90-mm and above)	ANTI-TANK GUIDED WEAPON LAUNCHERS (Crew served and/or mounted)	ARTILLERY/MORTARS (tubes 100-mm and above including Rocket Launchers)	ARMORED PERSONNEL CARRIERS & INFANTRY FIGHTING VEHICLES	ATTACK HELICOPTERS
86 / 176	13,500 / 42,600	12,300 / 32,200	11,000 / 35,000	33,000 / 75,000	560 / 960

NOTES: Warsaw Pact Divisions normally consist of fewer personnel than many NATO Divisions but contain more tanks and artillery, thereby obtaining similar combat power.

Warsaw Pact totals exclude the 17 Strategic Reserve Divisions in the Moscow, Volga and Ural Military Districts.

Early reinforcements for NATO are shown in the NATO/Warsaw Pact Force Comparison chart on the opposite page.

[1] Excludes France and Spain.

Number of Short-Range Nuclear Forces (SNF) at End of 1983[1]

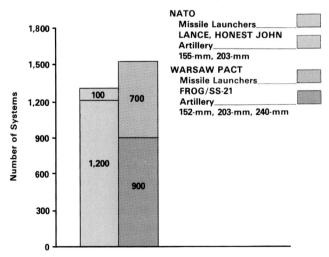

NATO
Missile Launchers ____
LANCE, HONEST JOHN
Artillery ____
155-mm, 203-mm
WARSAW PACT
Missile Launchers ____
FROG/SS-21
Artillery ____
152-mm, 203-mm, 240-mm

[1] For NATO the data reflect forces deployed in NATO Europe; for the Warsaw Pact forces facing NATO Europe. Excludes France and Spain.

Land-Based INF Aircraft in 1983[1]

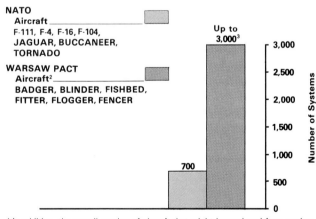

NATO
Aircraft ____
F-111, F-4, F-16, F-104,
JAGUAR, BUCCANEER,
TORNADO
WARSAW PACT
Aircraft[2] ____
BADGER, BLINDER, FISHBED,
FITTER, FLOGGER, FENCER

[1] In addition, the overall number of aircraft that might be equipped for a nuclear role are: about 1,900 for NATO and about 7,500 for the Warsaw Pact. Excludes France and Spain.
[2] The BACKFIRE bomber has been included in the strategic section because it has an inherent inter-continental capability although in its maritime and European land-attack roles it poses a serious threat to NATO Europe.
[3] In nuclear role.

Chapter IV

Sustainability, Readiness and Mobility

Soviet weapons systems alone do not present a comprehensive picture of the strong national commitment made by the Soviets to military power. The Soviets have not only gone to great lengths to build up and modernize all aspects of their forces, they have also comprehensively planned for the protection of key personnel, developed extensive logistics bases, undertaken large-scale training programs to maintain a high degree of readiness and expanded their strategic mobility capabilities. From the Soviet perspective, even in peacetime, the USSR's highly visible forces and their equipment are insufficient to achieve national objectives unless they are properly trained and can be commanded, moved and supplied.

Underlying Soviet military power is a complex mobilization and logistics support system designed to focus the resources of the entire nation on waging war. Soviet military planners emphasize that the Armed Forces must be prepared to participate in any type of conflict, ranging from short local wars to global conflicts of protracted duration. As a consequence, the Soviets have developed plans, established procedures and undertaken wide-ranging preparations to mobilize and sustain their forces under a variety of wartime contingencies. Parallel to the growth and modernization of strategic and theater combat forces has been the development of requisite support systems and resources. Soviet efforts have centered on creating and maintaining a

The mobilization and logistics systems supporting Soviet forces are designed to sustain strategic and theater forces in all combat contingencies. Even the largest main battle tanks of combat-ready mechanized units in the USSR can be rapidly delivered to forward theater areas on MAZ-537 heavy equipment transporters.

mobilization system extending into every area of Soviet life; a trained military manpower base for expanding the active forces and replacing losses; and a logistics system incorporating all classes of consumable supplies, war reserve equipment and well-equipped transport, repair, construction and medical units.

sions of Czechoslovakia and Afghanistan, or general, in which the entire nation prepares for war.

To draw rapidly on Soviet manpower and materiel during mobilization, the USSR has established an extensive network of mobilization offices known as military commissariats.

Il-76/CANDID military transports, with 4,600-kilometer range and 125-paratroop capacity, contribute to the USSR's increasing capability to transport personnel, arms and equipment to any area in the world.

Mobilization System: The USSR has established a national mobilization system that integrates the military, government, economy and general population. Military mobilization is undertaken to move the Armed Forces from a peacetime to a wartime footing. It includes bringing units up to full strength and readiness, militarizing selected civilian resources and creating new units. Soviet military mobilization is geared not only to the rapid build-up and wartime commitment of military units and resources, but also provides for the extended and selected mobilization of assets over time. Mobilization may be limited, such as that conducted in preparation for the inva-

These offices are located throughout the USSR and are subordinate to the General Staff. There are no counterparts in the United States. Their functions combine those of US draft boards, Armed Forces Reserve Centers and the Veterans Administration. In their areas of jurisdiction, the more than 4,000 commissariats maintain registers of all individuals eligible for conscription, all reservists liable for call-up and all equipment from the national economic sector—motor transport, engineer, repair, signal, medical and other materiel—designated for military use. This equipment is regularly inspected by commissariat representatives. In addition, the plans developed by the commissariats to call upon these resources in a crisis or war are closely coordinated with national economic plans.

Mobilization is initiated through military command channels. While military units begin preparations, the commissariats simultaneously execute their mobilization plans. Reservists are notified, assembled and dispatched to units or assignment points, with equipment likewise withdrawn from the national economy and integrated into the forces. In a general mobilization, the process could bring several million reservists and tens of thousands of trucks and other equipment into action in a few days. Additionally, entire support systems of the national economy can be quickly brought under military control. These include the rail system, the civil airline Aeroflot, the merchant fleet and elements of the national communications system.

Military Manpower Base: Soviet law requires universal male military service comprising active and reserve duty. This has established a military manpower base in which able-bodied male citizens between 18 and 50 years of age are either on active duty or subject to reserve service. As a consequence, the USSR today has a military manpower pool of about 50 million reservists, of whom some nine million have completed their active duty service within the last 5 years. These recently discharged reservists alone are more than adequate to meet initial mobilization needs and provide a substantial pool of additional personnel to replace or to create new units. Through the use of conscription, Soviet men are obligated to serve 2 years or, in the case of naval personnel aboard ship, 3 years of active service. As a result, of the total number of men in uniform in the Soviet force structure, 75 percent are conscripts. In addition, during a national mobilization for war, women, by law, would be inducted into the Armed Forces to fill staff positions, thereby releasing males for combat. Overall, the USSR military manpower base clearly reflects the Soviet view that future wars would require enormous manpower reserves.

Logistics: Soviet military planners have stressed the need to establish the logistics infrastructure and resources necessary to support high-intensity military operations by all components of their forces. To meet the logistics requirements, Soviet planners have prestocked large quantities of supplies in for-

ward areas for initial campaigns and created large strategic reserves for sustained conflicts. The USSR has made extensive logistics preparations both in designated theaters of military operations beyond Soviet borders and throughout the USSR itself.

In Eastern Europe and the military districts of the Western USSR, priority has been placed on prestocking critical ammunition and fuel reserves. Over the last decade, Soviet ammunition stocks intended to support combat operations against NATO in Central Europe have doubled in size. Large increases in Soviet military fuel stocks opposite Central Europe have also taken place. Additionally, each of the USSR Warsaw Pact Allies maintains substantial stockpiles of key military items, with provisions made for all Warsaw Pact forces to draw on civilian fuel stocks as well. Overall, theater logistics stockpiles in Eastern Europe and the border military districts of the USSR are capable of supporting Warsaw Pact military operations against NATO for 60 to 90 days.

Similar prepositioning of logistics stocks has taken place in the Soviet Far East. In this area, long, vulnerable lines of communication and the need to support large theater forces opposite China and Japan have resulted in an ambitious Soviet effort to build and expand their logistics base. Ammunition, fuel and other logistics stockpiles have increased over the last 15 years and continue to increase today. It is clear that the USSR has sought to establish the dedicated in-place logistics stockpiles necessary to support Soviet Far Eastern forces for at least the initial period of a major theater conflict. Far East ammunition and fuel stocks could sustain Soviet theater forces for perhaps 2 months, a sustainability potential nearing that of Warsaw Pact forces opposite NATO.

While Soviet planners believe that military objectives in some theaters may be achieved within weeks, additional logistics resources, termed strategic reserves, have been established for protracted operations. Many strategic reserve depots are concentrated in the interior military districts of the Soviet Union and would be used to support theater operations as required. Other strategic reserve depots store various types of military materiel, including spare parts, clothing, rations and medical supplies.

The USSR has placed in storage major

weapon systems and other war-fighting equipment. These items include tanks, armored personnel carriers, field artillery, air defense weaponry and maintenance, engineer, signal and other types of support equipment. Many of these systems, while older models, are capable of performing effectively in combat. They would be used to replace losses and create additional combat and support units. This equipment thus constitutes an important addition to Soviet military power.

To move supplies, repair damaged equipment, build and maintain lines of communication and treat personnel casualties, the USSR has deployed a variety of well-equipped logistics units with its forces in Eastern Europe and the USSR. These logistics assets are to be greatly expanded by the mobilization of personnel and materiel from the national economy. Motor transport units, many of which are kept loaded with ammunition and fuel during peacetime, possess large numbers of the most modern trucks. These include the very capable KAMAZ trucks, built with Western technology and assistance. Tactical pipeline construction units add substantially to fuel transport capabilities. Soviet pipe laying units are capable of laying approximately 80 kilometers of pipe per day using the TUM automatic pipe layer, or about 30 kilometers per day if done manually. The high pipe laying rate is in concert with Soviet offensive doctrine, which stipulates that armies are to advance at the rate of approximately 100 kilometers a day. Current Soviet stocks of available pipe for operations against the NATO central region are estimated to be about 12,000 kilometers of pipe. Equipment repair units are also highly mobile and designed to move forward with rapidly advancing combat formations. To facilitate the movement of combat and support forces, the USSR has bridge, rail and road construction units that would maintain key lines of communication at strategic and tactical levels. Medical units trained to treat and evacuate casualties are also an integral part of the Soviet Union's logistics system.

There are some 12,000 kilometers of pipeline with logistics units in Eastern Europe.

Major Soviet Military Storage Areas

Ammunition Depots

10 million metric tons arms/ammunition
including storage in Eastern Europe

Reserve Artillery Storage Depots

18,000 artillery and AAA pieces
including storage in Eastern Europe

Reserve Armor Storage Depots

8,000 armored vehicles (tanks/APCs)
including storage in Eastern Europe

Bridge Equipment Storage Depots

27,000 meters of bridging materials
including storage in Eastern Europe

**Petroleum, Oil and Lubricants
Storage Depot Concentrations**

52 million metric tons including
storage in Eastern Europe

Nuclear Warhead Stockpile Concentrations
Including storage in Eastern Europe

Overall, the USSR has invested very heavily in the mobilization and logistics support systems that are the underpinnings of Soviet military capabilities. Soviet military mobilization and logistics plans, critical elements in waging war, reflect their concepts for the conduct of theater-strategic offensive operations. These peacetime preparations indicate that the USSR has every intention of meeting the demanding support requirements associated with major conflicts that, in the Soviet view, could be protracted.

Readiness

In addition to providing for the protection of the national command authority, developing an extensive logistics support base and planning a national mobilization program, Soviet military doctrine demands that the Armed Forces be maintained at a high state of combat readiness. This ensures their expeditious deployment under any conditions. The Soviets are aware, however, that it is an economic burden to maintain peacetime forces that are fully deployed in the strength required for war. Therefore, in peacetime, some Soviet units are at full strength, while other units are ready for rapid deployment after mobilization and training.

The Soviets have taken very deliberate steps to ensure that their total force readiness is consistent with their perception of the threat, in addition to providing a flexible response capability. As noted, they have a tried and proven mobilization system with the requisite manpower to bring all units to their war personnel levels.

The Soviets have identified units that can be manned below wartime authorized levels with older but still effective equipment. Soviet forces in Eastern Europe opposite NATO are, however, maintained at high states of preparedness. These forces have modern equipment, constantly undergo a rigorous training program and are regularly drilled in new operational concepts.

The reorganization of Soviet air and ground elements has ensured a peacetime organization that is more closely aligned with their wartime personnel needs.

The survivability of Soviet weapons systems and personnel is enhanced by a very comprehensive dispersal system that would be executed during the transition to war. Once alerted, Soviet and non-Soviet Warsaw Pact units would deploy to areas that would decrease their vulnerability to detection and nuclear weapons. Aircraft would be flown to alternate airfields or specially prepared stretches of highways. Surface ships and submarines would depart from their main operating bases. Personnel, equipment and spare missiles needed for a refire capability of ICBMs would move to field locations. Alternate command posts have been constructed and are maintained in peacetime. Redundant, hardened and mobile communication links have been established. The placement of all Soviet forces in peacetime and preparations for dispersal at the outbreak of war reflect the Soviets' perceived threat and anticipated employment of forces in war.

Strategic Mobility

The Soviet Union, for decades a continental military power, now possesses an increased capability to transport personnel, arms and equipment to any area of the world. The demonstrated willingness and ability of the Soviets to employ strategically mobile forces in support of their goals and objectives have increased the potential for Soviet power projection into areas of vital Western interest. While the USSR is still behind the United States and its Allies in strategic mobility capability, the Soviet Armed Forces are dedicating high priority to closing this gap.

Current Soviet strategic movement capability is the culmination of 20 years of development. This has encompassed:

• formation of strategically mobile forces and military transport assets,

• modernization and expansion of civilian transport modes that are easily mobilized and adapted to military transport requirements, and

• establishment of national-level planning and management bodies that can assemble the necessary strategic lift assets from both military and civilian sectors to meet strategic transport requirements.

Soviet strategic mobility is based, in part, on amphibious assault ships and increasingly capable military air and land transport forces. These military forces are supplemented by a large reserve of modern civilian air, sea and land transport systems. This Soviet system of peacetime preparation and wartime planning for employment of transport assets and associated personnel from the civilian sector is integrated. The Soviet leadership has established detailed procedures for mobilizing civilian transport resources for military employment and routinely uses these assets in a variety of military exercises and contingencies. Transportation management is consolidated at the Ministry of Defense level under Marshal of the Soviet Union S.K. Kurkotkin, Senior Logistician of the Armed Forces and a Deputy Minister of Defense. One of the directorates subordinate to Marshal Kurkotkin is tasked with managing transport assets available from the military and civilian sectors.

The most visible asset of Soviet strategic mobility is the military air transport force known as VTA. In wartime, VTA would trans-port airborne and air assault troops and provide logistics airlift to the Armed Forces. In peacetime, VTA aircraft are frequently seen on the airfields of Third World client states where they are involved in arms and equipment deliveries. This force, composed of about 600 aircraft, has shown continuing improvement in range, speed and cargo capacity as more modern jet transports enter the inventory. More than half the VTA holdings consist of the four-engine, propeller-driven An-12/CUBs, with highly capable Il-76/CANDID long-range jet transports being added at the rate of about 30 per year. The Il-76 constitutes more than a third of the total VTA inventory. Soviet heavy-lift An-22/COCK transports include 55 aircraft. Production of the new

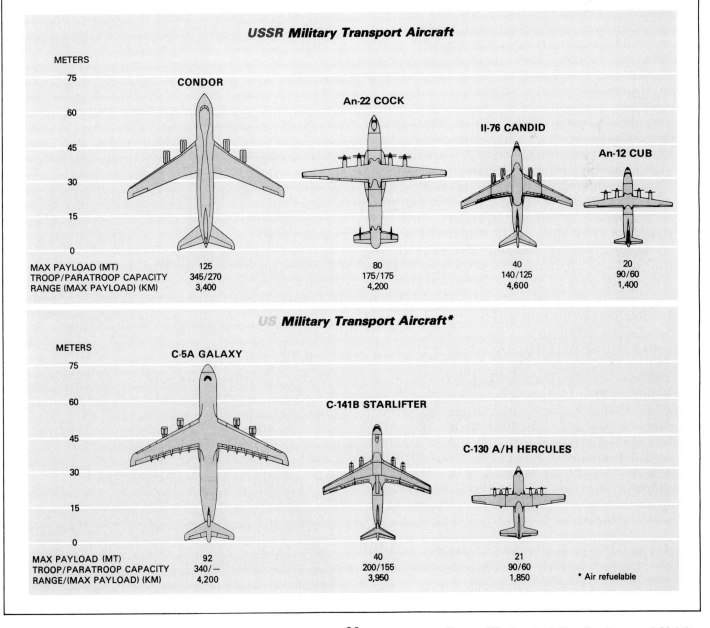

USSR Military Transport Aircraft

	CONDOR	An-22 COCK	Il-76 CANDID	An-12 CUB
MAX PAYLOAD (MT)	125	80	40	20
TROOP/PARATROOP CAPACITY	345/270	175/175	140/125	90/60
RANGE (MAX PAYLOAD) (KM)	3,400	4,200	4,600	1,400

US Military Transport Aircraft*

	C-5A GALAXY	C-141B STARLIFTER	C-130 A/H HERCULES
MAX PAYLOAD (MT)	92	40	21
TROOP/PARATROOP CAPACITY	340/—	200/155	90/60
RANGE/(MAX PAYLOAD) (KM)	4,200	3,950	1,850

* Air refuelable

heavy-lift CONDOR transport, comparable to the US C-5A GALAXY and scheduled for deployment in the 1987-88 timeframe, will substantially improve and expand VTA's heavy-lift capability. Availability of the CONDOR will help offset some of the problems the Soviets occasionally face in obtaining overflight and transit rights in foreign countries.

Soviet capacity to airlift troops rises significantly with the mobilization of over 1,000 medium- and long-range aircraft belonging to the State-owned Aeroflot airline. Use of civilian transport aircraft such as the Il-62 and Il-86 provides the Soviets an immediate source of strategic air transport. Military and civil transport aviation provides an excellent illustration of the close interrelationship of the Soviet military establishment and civil sectors. For example, the Minister of Civil Aviation is an active duty senior general officer. Additionally, several key ministry members are active duty officers, and most civilian air crews serving with Aeroflot hold reserve military commissions.

Soviet strategic sealift capability is based on approximately 80 navy ships. The Soviets depend primarily on the large USSR merchant fleet for strategic sealift. This fleet has grown steadily for the past two decades. The Soviet merchant fleet is the most militarily adaptable in the world and the foundation of Soviet strategic mobility in general. It is composed of more than 1,700 ships with a combined deadweight tonnage of more than 20 million tons, an increase of more than 500 percent in the past 20 years. Almost half the cargo ships in the fleet have cranes capable of lifting heavy military vehicles. The Soviets emphasize construction of merchant vessels that not only have commercial value but also can be adapted quickly to military use. The Soviet merchant fleet is used regularly to replenish naval combatants. The fleet now has more than 50 roll-on/roll-off barge carriers and specialized roll-on/float-off and rail transport vessels. It provides Soviet planners with the means to transport Soviet forces to remote areas of the world. The merchant fleet is used today to transport arms and the forces of client states in support of Soviet power projection objectives.

Soviet military sealift now includes two units of the 14,000-ton IVAN ROGOV-Class amphibious assault transport docks.

85   Chapter IV   Sustainability, Readiness and Mobility

A river-sea fleet of some 700 ships augments the ocean-going merchant fleet. These ships operate on the Soviet and European inland waterway system and in coastal sea routes. Frequently used to transport military cargo in peacetime, these ships represent a means of wartime transport that could be used in a number of potential theaters.

Merchant tanker refuels KRIVAK-Class frigate.

In the last 20 years, the USSR has expanded its military inventory of heavy equipment transporters, in particular, the MAZ-537 tractor with a 50 metric ton capacity trailer. The Soviets currently have more than 3,500 heavy equipment transporters available for military operations. Combat forces from the Soviet interior can be transported rapidly to forward areas opposite NATO and China to augment the large forces already in place.

Rail remains the primary transport mode for forces opposite NATO and China. The entire Soviet rail system is organized along quasi-military lines. Military mobilization of its civilian equipment and operating personnel can be completed in a matter of a few days. Thousands of locomotives and tens of thousands of pieces of rolling stock would thus be immediately available to support Soviet wartime operations.

Soviet theater and strategic movement capabilities that have been developing since the early 1960s, represent a clear challenge to Western defense planners. Their strength and capacity are based on the ability to increase quickly military transport potential through utilization of the civilian transport sector. The impact of such a mobilization effort on the Soviet economy would cause severe disruption of the normal transportation of goods and services within and between cities. Nonetheless, Soviet peacetime planning and preparation for wartime employment of the military and civilian transport assets are a major strength and a key element in understanding Soviet military power.

US Logistics

The US maintains slightly about one million personnel in the Selected Reserve and about 400,000 Individual Ready Reserves. The Selected Reserve, consisting of National Guard and Reserve units, constitutes approximately 45 percent of the total force structure. Although Selected Reserve manning has im-

MAZ-537 tractor-trailers, loaded with tanks, in convoy.

proved significantly in recent years, it will not approach the numbers of trained reserves in the USSR. US Selected Reserves include:

- one-third of the Army's combat divisions,
- one-half of the nation's strategic airlift crews,
- one-third of the Military Airlift Command's aeromedical evacuation aircrews, and
- an additional Marine Division and Air Wing

Prepositioning of US equipment in Europe began in the 1960s in response to US and European concerns that the forces in the theater were inadequate to meet the Warsaw Pact threat. Under the POMCUS program, the Army has prepositioned in Europe heavy equipment for four divisions and supporting units, and will soon provide equipment for two more divisions. The Air Force prepositions rapid runway repair equipment, ground support equipment, munitions, fuel and other consumables. The levels of prepositioned fuel and munitions, however, continue to fall short of objectives.

The US goal is to possess sufficient war reserve stocks to sustain wartime activity until industrial production can provide the required support. The US objective is to correct the NATO-Warsaw Pact sustainability imbalance by the 1990s.

US Readiness

Over the past 3 years, the readiness of US combat units and equipment has improved significantly, particularly in aircraft and ship spares and repair parts. Increased flying hours and steaming hours translate directly into increased combat capability. Notwithstanding gains made by the Services, shortfalls in critical personnel categories, medical support, spare parts, munitions, training funds, chemical defense and survivable command, control, communications and intelligence (C³I) support capabilities continue to inhibit readiness.

In recognition of the need for realistic and challenging training, the Services have developed training centers and ranges using both field exercises and simulators to improve the combat readiness of US Armed Forces. Cooperative training projects with our NATO Allies enhance standardization of tactics and procedures. As an extension of training, US

forces participate in approximately 60 exercises each year throughout the world to test and evaluate combined systems and lines of communications. During 1983, these exercises included BRIGHT STAR in the Middle East, REFORGER in Germany, TEAM SPIRIT in Korea and AHUAS TARA II with our friends and Allies in the Central American and the Caribbean region.

US Strategic Mobility

The US capability to move troops and equipment by air is unmatched by any country in the world. US airlift assets include the transports of the Military Airlift Command (MAC) augmented by the Civil Reserve Air Fleet (CRAF) in time of emergency. Current MAC strategic mobility transports include 70 C-5 and 234 C-141 aircraft. Under the CRAF program, US civilian airlines augment the military with an additional 108 cargo and 212 intercontinental passenger aircraft. The combined cargo carrying capability of these US aircraft is more than twice that of the Soviet Union's military and civilian aircraft. However, when distance to a region of possible conflict is considered, this 2:1 ratio favoring US cargo capacity can change significantly in terms of maximum number of tons deliverable per day.

US sealift capability, even more than airlift, is dependent on the civil sector. The Military Sealift Command currently owns or has under charter 31 dry cargo ships that would be available for military contingencies. Another 18 ships are fully loaded and ready to sail immediately upon notification for use in any overseas location. The MSC fleet could be augmented within 10 days with 32 ships currently in the Ready Reserve Force of the National Defense Reserve Fleet (NDRF). While the 154 ships in the NDRF would be activated over a several-month time period, the bulk of early US sealift would come from the 224 militarily useful ships in the US merchant marine fleet. Taken together, these fleets total 459 dry cargo ships with a deadweight tonnage of about 7.5 million tons or about one-third of the total Soviet fleet deadweight tonnage.

The maintenance of modern strategic mobility forces will, for the foreseeable future, make an essential contribution to our national security and the security of friends and Allies throughout the Free World.

Chapter V

Soviet Military-Industrial Complex

The Soviet priority attached to military power has required a national commitment to a dedicated and militarily oriented industrial system. The past 35 years have shown a tremendous growth in all sectors of Soviet military industries and the tightly integrated national strategy of military production, from mining of raw materials to the fabrication of finished weapons systems.

Critical Industries

The dramatic increases in Soviet metals production underscore the USSR's priority of establishing a solid industrial base. Historically, the Soviets have developed their reserve of strategic minerals, and continued expansion of this base has guaranteed their independence from foreign manipulation. Recent introduction of modern processing and fabricating techniques has further strengthened industrial independence.

Traditionally, the Soviet industrial system has projected an image of quantity over quality. Recently, the Soviets have designated sectors in each basic industry to develop the best state-of-the-art materials for advanced weapons systems. These sectors receive priority for scientists, equipment, research support and incentives. They are also controlled and operated by the military ministries. Industries producing weaponry, such as ICBMs, nuclear warheads, bombers and submarines are totally merged with producers of strategic metals such as titanium, aluminum and beryllium.

In the aluminum industry, the Ministry of

At Nikolayev Shipyard, overhead cranes with a combined lift of more than 1,000 tons frame the construction of the Soviet Navy's first nuclear-powered aircraft carrier — to be fitted with catapults and arresting gear for the operation of high-performance jet aircraft. The fourth unit of the 37,000-ton KIEV-Class carriers fits out, at left.

Aviation Industry, a defense ministry, runs the metal fabrication plants. These plants are designed to produce components for aerospace industries and are located in proximity to the final assembly plants, although the aluminum must often be obtained from suppliers thousands of miles away. The plants have excess capacities and employ advanced forging and fabricating technologies that are among the best in the world. This system streamlines component production and delivery to assembly plants, assuring consistency in aerospace programs.

The titanium industry provides a unique insight into Soviet dedication to developing high-risk industry for the manufacture of large-scale military equipment. Its production and technological growth have been heavily influenced by the production of titanium-hulled submarines. As a result, Soviet processing and fabricating technology of thick plate titanium is at least 10 years ahead of that in the United States, allowing for the construction of the fastest and deepest diving attack submarine, the ALFA.

Energy

As with strategic minerals self-sufficiency, the USSR is also the only major industrial nation that is energy independent. It is the world's foremost producer of petroleum and has the largest proven oil reserves outside the Persian Gulf. Soviet oil exports are second only to those of Saudi Arabia. Soviet natural gas reserves and exports are by far the largest in the world and last year enabled them to overtake the United States as the world's largest natural gas producer. While not growing currently, coal production is based on the largest reserves in the world.

An estimated 20 percent of the USSR's total capital investment now goes to energy development, an increase from about 15 percent during the past Five-Year Plan. The fuel and energy base continues to expand and provide surplus quantities of these most valuable commodities for the foreseeable future. Industry has historically accounted for approximately 60 percent of total energy consumed, and the percentage is not expected to go down. Though dedicated primarily to supporting the military and military-related industries, the Soviet energy base also earns over $19 billion annually in convertible or hard currency through the sale of oil, natural gas, coal and electric power, accounting for more than 55 percent of total Soviet export earnings. In addition, the Soviet Union supplies the bulk of Eastern Europe's energy requirements. Energy exports to Western Europe provide the Soviet Union economic leverage, with implications for NATO unity.

The electric power industry, coupled with Soviet natural resources, has been the basis for industrialization of the USSR. Electric power consumption for industrial use is nearly the same as in the United States even though the United States has nearly twice the generating capacity. This demonstrates the Soviet willingness to subordinate the consumer sector to the needs of industry, especially that which supports the military. Military-industrial installations generally are served by the national power system or collocated plants, and a system of strict priorities ensures an adequate supply of electricity during times of emergency.

US Industrial Base

The national industrial base encompasses the total industrial capacity to produce and maintain goods in the United States. The defense industrial base refers to the industrial capacity, both in the private and public sectors, available to produce and support military materiel required for the Armed Forces. A very small percentage of the defense industrial base is Government-owned since, in accordance with legislative mandate, the United States places maximum reliance on the private sector for the production of defense goods. There are between 25,000 and 30,000 private sector prime contractors throughout the United States doing business with the Department of Defense, while the Government owns only 72 defense production plants, of which 14 are in "lay-away" status for emergency use. Since 1965, there has been only one Government-owned plant for production of defense goods constructed in the United States, and modernization of existing plants has been very limited. In addition, the US private sector has, in recent years, lagged behind most other major industrialized nations in modernization and technological improvements of key heavy industries.

Soviet military production facilities are kept active and have the capability for rapid expansion in wartime. Many items produced by the Soviets can be simplified by removing technologically sophisticated sub-systems, resulting in their ability to produce larger quantities of less complex weapons. By contrast, US reliance on high-technology weapons, combined with a decline in heavy industry and traditional manufacturing methods, constricts the US ability to expand its production capability rapidly in a major crisis.

In contrast to the stability and growth in the Soviet defense industries, business in the US sector has been cyclical and has led to instability in the industry. During 1980 and 1981, numerous studies and reports documented the deterioration of the national industrial base. Findings included factors such as declining productivity growth, aging facilities, material shortages, increasing foreign dependency, skilled labor shortages and often burdensome Government regulations. The result was a dramatic decline in the number of defense contractors. For example, from 1967 to 1981, the total number of companies involved in aerospace production declined from 6,000 to 3,500; of that 3,500, 1,500 had entered the market since 1979. Since the late 1960s, employment in the US aircraft industry decreased by 200,000 or 25 percent.

To reverse this alarming trend and to counteract the rapidly growing Soviet threat, the US has taken actions that are beginning to result in industrial expansion and modernization. These include establishment of the Department of Defense Acquisition Improvement Program to streamline procedures and make defense contracting a more attractive business venture, assistance to the educational community in identifying and solving present and potential skilled labor shortages and improvement in planning by making available to industry data that project 5-year defense requirements and show the impact of defense spending in 400 industrial sectors.

The Science and Technology (S&T) Program of the Department of Defense, augmented by the efforts of other Federal agencies and the private sector, provides the basis for the development and fielding of future weapons systems and equipment. The United States does not seek to match the Soviet Union soldier for soldier or weapon for weapon. Reliance is placed on superior technology and, most particularly, the ability to apply that technology to superior weapons systems to offset quantitative disadvantages. Superior technology can offset numerical inferiority within reason,

but as the Soviets continue to increase their R&D efforts, this technological advantage is being reduced. Therefore, actions to develop and maintain an effective and efficient S&T base upon which to ensure our national security are of paramount importance.

Military Production

The USSR has dedicated a larger share of its natural and industrial resources, year after year, to the production of military weapons than any other country in peacetime. For decades Soviet industry has manufactured a complete range of military weaponry and support equipment in very large quantities. These extraordinary output levels have been achieved

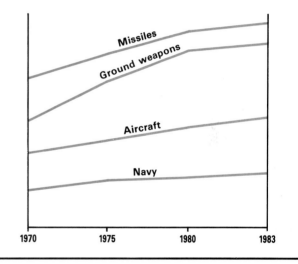

Soviet Military Production Facilities— Growth of Floorspace

by massive investments of money, raw materials and manpower, not only in military equipment but in the plants, factories and shipyards required to support weapons programs. These programs are still evolving. First, there is a thrust to produce more capable weapons and equipment. Second, the Soviet Union is expanding existing factories, building new ones and providing, on a priority basis, new and modern manufacturing technologies to the industries supporting military-related production. Finally, it is further integrating its military-industrial complex with those of Eastern Europe.

The Soviet drive toward increased weapons sophistication and military industrial modernization has caused them to reduce the planned number of weapons systems produced annually and to extend the procurement cycle. The ongoing expansion and modernization of the Soviet industrial base as well as sustained high levels of activity in R&D field indicate, however, that production of sophisticated military materiel will not only continue but will probably increase in the future.

The nuclear-powered TYPHOON and DELTA III ballistic missile submarines and OSCAR-Class cruise missile attack submarines are among the units built on multiple assembly ways in the extremely large construction halls of Severodvinsk, the world's largest submarine production yard.

The TYPHOON-Class 25,000-ton strategic ballistic missile submarine.

The vast number of military-industrial facilities ensures Soviet procurement goals. Today, there are over 150 factories and shipyards turning out weapons, armored vehicles, ships, aircraft, missiles, ammunition and explosives, while another 150 plants provide vital combat support items such as radar, trucks and signal equipment. These facilities are supported by thousands of component and parts plants. This post-World War II industrial base has been expanded and modernized. Since 1970, the major weapons plants have nearly doubled in size. The Soviet Union's reliance upon tanks as the prime ground force weapon system is well highlighted by the continuous expansion of that segment of the industry.

The growth of the facilities dedicated to naval and aerospace weapons production has been extraordinary. At Severodvinsk Shipyard, the world's largest submarine production yard, shop space has increased by several hundred thousand square meters, approximately 80 percent since 1965. Moreover, Severodvinsk is one of five Soviet yards producing submarines. The 24 naval construction yards that produce the bulk of naval ships show a 30 percent increase, or over 125,000 square meters of new building ways, since 1970.

Despite the proven capabilities of the Soviet aircraft industry to turn out large numbers of military aircraft annually, further expansion and modernization of aircraft plants are underway. For example, a new aircraft plant is currently under construction at Ulyanovsk to produce larger aircraft such as bombers and heavy-lift transport aircraft.

The Soviet leadership is committed to providing large quantities of modern military equipment in peacetime as well as to increasing production rapidly in times of crisis.

Soviet Industrial Modernization

The Soviet Communist Party leadership has given added political impetus to industrial modernization programs for the introduction of new manufacturing technologies in all sectors of the military-industrial complex. They are increasingly dependent upon automation and computerization. Introduction of computers into Soviet military production represents a long-standing goal first stated in the 1960s. Programs initiated during the 1970s have already resulted in the introduction of thousands of computer-aided design and automated production process control systems, with more planned. Party leaders have strongly endorsed the next step of linking together more sophisticated machine tools and robots at production facilities. This promises the establishment of more integrated and technologically flexible manufacturing environments ideally suited for the production of highly sophisticated weaponry. Integrated computer-aided design systems in this high-technology environment will link the scientific research, experimental design, prototype and series production stages of the Soviet weapons programs. This will result in significant efficiencies in terms of development times, availability of skilled manpower and material resources, as well as plant and equipment, all of which are critical factors in meeting future Soviet weapons needs. The impact of technology transfer on the Soviet R&D program is examined in the following chapter.

Production Capability

To place the USSR's military-industrial complex in perspective, a brief review of the capability to produce major weapons systems is warranted.

Ground Force Equipment

The Soviet Union is the world's largest producer of army materiel. As with all types of military equipment, Soviet production has in recent years emphasized quality as well as quantity.

Tanks and Armored Vehicles: Last year, the USSR produced 2,700 tanks and approximately 4,500 other armored fighting vehicles. Tank production increased by nearly 10 percent in 1983 over 1982. Output included the T-72—in its 10th year of serial production—and the newer T-80 class of tanks. The tank plant in Nizhniy Tagil is supported by at least three other tank plants in Kharkov, Omsk and Chelyabinsk. Additionally, T-72s are produced in Eastern Europe. As the T-80 has shifted to full-scale series production, output has grown from a 1981 low. Further increases are to be expected.

The output of other armored vehicles includes nine different types manufactured at seven Soviet plants as well as at two factories in Eastern Europe. The most important of these are the BMP infantry combat vehicle (ICV), the BMD airborne ICV, the BTR-60 armored personnel carrier (APC), and the

Main battle tank production including, top to bottom, the T-62, T-64, T-72 and T-80 has led to a continued increase in Soviet tank force size and armored capabilities.

BRDM-2 armored reconnaissance vehicle. Currently, the latter two are made only for export. Soviet production of the wheeled BTR-70 APC ended in 1982 although some, as well as additional BMPs, are being imported from other Warsaw Pact nations. While BMPs have been in production for more than a decade in the USSR, the United States only began to introduce a technologically equivalent vehicle, the BRADLEY, in 1981.

Artillery: Some 3,500 artillery pieces and multiple rocket launchers were produced in 1983. This included four towed pieces—the T-12 100-mm gun, the D-30 122-mm howitzer, the 152-mm field gun, and the 85-mm antitank gun. While output of these towed pieces declined slightly, production of five distinct self-propelled models, which range from 122-mm to a 203-mm, remained constant as did output of three models of the 122-mm rocket launchers and the larger 220-mm piece.

Production of antiaircraft artillery declined somewhat, and nearly all of the 23-mm self-propelled ZSU-23-4 AA guns were destined for export. However, a newer follow-on to the ZSU-23-4 entered production. Most artillery production is accomplished at plants in Sverdlovsk and Perm, even though as many as nine plants have been recently associated with such production.

Helicopters: The Soviet Union, which continues to turn out a substantial number of helicopters—over 800 per year in 1982 and 1983—has achieved great success in helicopter design and production. The Soviets have the distinction of having produced the largest and most heavily armed helicopters in the world, the Mi-26/HALO and the Mi-8/HIP E, respectively. Five helicopters are known to be in production—HIP, HIND, HALO, HAZE and HELIX—while at least two or three new models are believed to be in prototype testing. There are five airframe plants that produce helicopters in the USSR. The Mi-8/HIP, which is built at two plants in Kazan and Ulan Ude, is still being produced in the largest quantity. Over 10,000 HIPs have been produced, including four new specialized military variants plus two major modifications. Over 1,500 antitank Mi-24/HIND have been produced at plants in Arsenyev and Rostov for the Soviet forces and for export. Since 1980, two new helicopters have entered service, the heavy-lift Mi-26/HALO, which is comparable to a C-130 transport aircraft in load and lift capability, and the ASW Ka-27/HELIX. A new attack helicopter, the HAVOC in the class of the US AH-64/Apache, also is believed to be in prototype testing and may enter production this year.

Ships

Soviet naval ship construction continued, with the trend toward progressively larger, more capable ships. For more than two decades, while the number of ships produced annually has declined, ship size and capability have increased for all types. The Soviet Union's extensive ship construction program continues to produce an entirely new generation of submarine and surface combatants.

Submarines: During 1983, 10 submarines were completed: Six were nuclear-powered attack submarines, one a ballistic missile submarine and three diesel-powered attack submarines. Construction of established program types included the following:

- five nuclear-powered attack submarines (SSNs),
- one nuclear-powered cruise missile attack submarine (SSGN),
- one nuclear-powered ballistic missile submarine (SSBN), and
- three attack submarines (SSs)

The first unit of two nuclear attack submarines, the MIKE and SIERRA-Classes, were launched in 1983, and an experimental nuclear submarine, the UNIFORM-Class, was completed at Sudomekh Shipyard in Leningrad. Four other shipyards—Admiralty, Gorkiy, Komsomolsk and Severodvinsk—are engaged in submarine production.

Surface Ships: Ten major surface combatants consisting of eight different classes were completed in 1983. Construction of established programs included the following: two UDALOY-Class guided missile destroyers (DDGs), a SOVREMENNYY-Class DDG, a KASHIN II-Class DDG for export, a KONI-Class frigate (FF) for export, four GRISHA-Class corvettes and more than 50 small combatants and auxiliaries. The keel was laid for the first Soviet conventional take-off-and-landing (CTOL) aircraft carrier early in 1983 at Nikolayev. The second KIROV-Class nuclear-powered guided missile cruiser (CGN) began sea trials, and construction started on a third unit at Leningrad's Baltic Shipyard.

The first SLAVA-Class guided missile cruiser (CG), provisionally identified in last year's

In ballistic missile submarine production, the YANKEE I, YANKEE II, DELTA I, DELTA II and DELTA III-Classes, top to bottom, have emerged from the USSR's building ways. The TYPHOON-Class is the most recent addition.

Soviet shipyards are producing a new generation of surface warships including, top to bottom, the nuclear-powered KIROV-Class guided missile cruiser, SOVREMENNYY-Class and UDALOY-Class guided missile destroyers and the SLAVA-Class guided missile cruiser.

edition as the KRASINA-Class, completed sea trials, and two additional units are under construction at Nikolayev. Guided missile destroyer (DDG) production increased to four units in 1983, as compared to one in 1982. Additionally, five units each of the SOVREMENNYY and UDALOY-Classes of DDG are known to be on the building ways or fitting out at Leningrad and Kaliningrad shipyards.

Fourteen additional shipyards are also engaged in the production of surface ships for the Soviet Navy.

Eastern Europe continued to contribute to Soviet naval power, providing additional ship construction. The non-Warsaw Pact countries have produced approximately 80 percent of the amphibious landing ships and roughly 40 percent of the naval auxiliaries.

Aircraft

The USSR is second only to the United States as a producer of aircraft. The high output of the aircraft industry has enabled the Soviets to maintain and constantly upgrade the world's largest air force and the world's largest state-owned civil air fleet. The USSR is a major exporter of civilian and military aircraft, thereby helping to extend its sphere of political, military and economic influence abroad.

Bombers: The Soviets have three strategic bombers in development or production: the BACKFIRE, the turboprop BEAR H and the new BLACKJACK. The BACKFIREs have been built at the large airframe plant in Kazan. Production of a new variant of the BEAR bomber, the BEAR H, is underway at the Taganrog plant. This aircraft has been assessed as the initial carrier of the AS-X-15 long-range cruise missile (ALCM). Development of the BLACKJACK continues. Full-scale BLACKJACK production is expected to take place in the new complex being added to the Kazan Airframe Plant.

Tactical Aircraft: Total Soviet fighter output numbered approximately 950 in 1983—a decline from around 1,300 in 1980. This decline resulted from a combination of factors: the decreased output from older long-running programs such as FLOGGER, FISHBED and FITTER, and the recent changeover to newer programs such as FOXHOUND, FULCRUM and FLANKER, which have yet to attain maximum production. Fighter production models include 10 different aircraft. In addition to the six models mentioned above, production of FOXBAT, FORGER, FROGFOOT and FENCER also continued. Although modern, state-of-the-art fighters are increasingly difficult and expensive to produce, it is anticipated that the Soviet hallmark of large quantity fighter output will be maintained for the foreseeable future.

Two new Soviet aircraft, the FOXHOUND interceptor and the FROGFOOT ground-attack aircraft—produced at Gorkiy and Tbilisi, respectively—have become operational with Soviet forces since early 1980. In addition, four improved variants of older Soviet fighter designs—two variants of FITTER and two of FENCER—also entered production during the 1980-83 time period. The latest Soviet fighters to enter production are the FULCRUM counter-air fighter-interceptor, at a plant in Moscow, and the FLANKER air-superiority aircraft at a plant in Komsomolsk. In addition, the Soviets have at least one new fighter, as well as variants of existing fighters in various stages of development and flight testing.

Transports: The Soviets fill all of their high-performance transport aircraft requirements from domestic production. About 75 of the 300 transports produced in 1983 were for the military, primarily the Il-76/CANDID and the An-26/CURL. The CANDID is built at the continuously expanding airframe plant in Tashkent. Other transports in production include CLASSIC, CRUSTY, CARELESS, CLOBBER, CAMBER and CLINE at six additional plants. The most important aircraft of this type under development is the CONDOR, with series production probably starting in 1987-88. The seven plants are expected to turn out an average of about 325 transports annually for the next several years.

Missiles

While missile production numbers are difficult to establish with precision, the estimated data on these pages are as authoritative as possible. The Soviet missile industry continues to receive a very high priority in Soviet military production. Consequently there has been continuous expansion and modernization of key missile producing facilities. The Soviets are not only producing increasingly advanced missiles but also have an impressive number of new missile classes. More than 20 plants produce missile systems for the

Soviet strategic forces include, top to bottom, the BISON, BEAR and BACKFIRE long-range strategic bombers, as well as the new BLACK-JACK bomber now in development.

Production of Ground Forces Materiel
USSR/NSWP and NATO[1]

Equipment Type	1979 USSR	1979 NSWP	1980 USSR	1980 NSWP	1981 USSR	1981 NSWP	1982 USSR	1982 NSWP	1983 USSR	1983 NSWP	1983 NATO
Tanks	3,500	800	3,100	700	2,000	520	2,500	600	2,700	550	1,650
Other Armored Fighting Vehicles	6,000	1,800	6,500	1,300	5,200	1,300	4,500	1,400	4,500	1,300	2,280
Towed Field Artillery	1,400	150	1,400	150	1,600	200	1,800	250	1,700	300	335
Self-Propelled Field Artillery	900	10	900	50	1,000	50	1,100	50	1,100	100	155
Multiple Rocket Launchers	600	150	700	150	700	150	700	100	700	100	95
Self-Propelled AA Artillery	300	100	300	100	300	50	200	50	100	0	0
Towed AA Artillery	—	200	—	150	—	250	—	200	—	225	125

[1] Revised to reflect current total production information. Includes United States, excludes France and Spain.

Armed Forces of the Soviet Union.

ICBMs: The Soviets continue to manufacturing liquid-propellant ICBMs. Total output of these ICBMs in 1983 was on the order of 150. In the future the Soviets are expected to develop and produce new types of liquid-propellant systems, as well as the two new solid-propellant systems (SS-X-24 and SS-X-25), now in pre-series production.

SLBMs: The Soviets continue to produce four SLBMs—the SS-N-6, SS-N-8, SS-N-17 and SS-N-18—at the rate of 200 a year. One new system, the SS-N-20/TYPHOON, is in series production. There are several plants engaged in SLBM production.

Cruise Missiles: The Soviets are building seven cruise missiles—the SS-N-2, SS-N-3, SS-N-7, SS-N-9, SS-N-12, SS-N-19 and SS-N-22—

at the annual rate of 800. This production stretches from plants in the Far East Maritime provinces to the Ukraine. In addition, three long-range, land-attack, nuclear-armed cruise missiles, as discussed in Chapter II, are being built.

SRINF/SNF: Production of SRINF and SNF missiles in the 1980s has been stepped up, increasing from 300 in 1979 to an assessed 350 in 1983. This increase has heralded a large-scale modernization program intended to replace the thousands of old, short-range ballistic missiles and unguided rockets (FROGs) with new, more accurate SS-21s and SS-23s as well as improved SS-12/22s.

New production capability in the USSR is available to support large-scale deployment of the SS-21 and SS-23 into the 1990s at an an-

Aircraft Production
USSR and NATO[1]

Aircraft Type	1979 USSR	1980 USSR	1981 USSR	1982 USSR	1983 USSR	1983 US
Bombers	30	30	30	35	35	0
Fighters/Fighter-Bombers	1,300	1,300	1,350	1,100	950	675
Transports	400	350	350	300	300	290
ASW	10	10	10	10	5	20
Helicopters	700	700	800	800	800	725
Utility/Trainers	100	85	50	50	35	425

[1] Revised to reflect current total production information. Includes United States, excludes France and Spain.

Missile Production
USSR and NATO[1]

Missile Type	1979 USSR	1980 USSR	1981 USSR	1982 USSR	1983 USSR	1983 NATO
ICBMs	225	250	200	175	150	0
LRINF	100	100	100	100	100	25
SRBMs	300	300	300	300	350	0
SLCMs	700	750	750	800	800	225
SLBMs	200	200	175	175	200	70
SAMs	53,000	53,000	53,000	53,000	55,000	6,000

[1] Revised to reflect current total production information. Includes United States, excludes France and Spain.

nual production rate of over 200 missiles.

SAMs: The Soviet Union produces the widest variety of strategic and tactical surface-to-air systems in the world. The newer SAM systems such as the SA-X-12 and the SA-10 and SA-11, both of which are in series

Naval Ship Construction USSR and NATO[1]

Ship Type	1979 USSR	1980 USSR	1981 USSR	1982 USSR	1983 USSR	1983 NATO
Submarines	12	13	11	8	10	8
Major Combatants	11	11	9	8	10	25
Minor Combatants	55	65	45	55	45	30
Auxiliaries	7	9	6	5	6	7

[1] Revised to reflect current total production information. Includes United States, excludes France and Spain.

production, represent sophisticated weapons systems. Currently, the Soviet Union produces more than 50,000 SAMs annually. There are about a dozen systems being produced at factories in Moscow, Leningrad, Sverdlovsk, Kirov and Kovrov.

Radar and Electronics
About 20 new radars are now undergoing development at Soviet test centers. Recently produced radars reflect the new technologies that have been in testing during the past decade. The Soviets have characteristically put large varieties and large numbers of specialized radars into production compared to Western military philosophy of fielding fewer kinds of systems and in fewer numbers.

In addition to mobile and transportable ground-based air defense radars, the Soviets continue their program of constructing large, fixed-site modern phased-array ballistic missile defense radars. These large phased-array radars will complement and supplement older operational ballistic missile warning radars allowing the Soviets more warning against potential enemy strategic strikes.

The ability of the Soviet Union to produce major weapons systems in the peacetime environment of today's world is unmatched by any nation. Their production programs and modernization efforts for both the means of production and equipment produced reflect

the highest national commitment to the Soviet defense establishment.

Military Expenditures
Over the past 10 years, the Soviets have built far more armaments than the United States. This is clearly reflected in the Soviet production of major weapons. For example, during this period, the Soviets produced three times the number of submarines, twice the number of tactical combat aircraft and four times the number of tanks that the United States produced. During this period—1973 to 1982—the dollar cost of Soviet procurement of arms and other military assets exceeded that of the United States by some $240 billion. The gap in fielded hardware that this represents could not soon be overcome even if the United States were to match Soviet arms investments. The dollar cost of Soviet procurement has leveled off since the mid-1970s at an annual amount substantially higher than the US level. The high level of Soviet investment in research and development, twice that of the United States, strongly suggests that the value of annual Soviet procurement efforts will soon begin to rise again as the many new

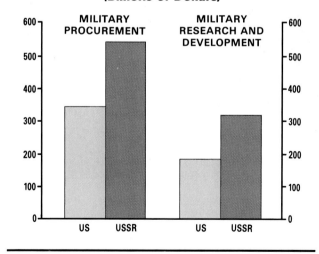

Ten-Year Selected Defense Cost Comparisons 1973-1982 (Billions of Dollars)

weapons now being tested move into full-scale production.

While the large investment of economic resources cannot be equated directly with military capabilities, estimates of the magnitude and growth of their military spending can provide a picture of the priority and level of ef-

fort that the Soviet leadership accords to the military. The estimates of the dollar cost of Soviet defense programs—that is, what the Soviet military establishment would cost if built and operated in the United States using US prices and wages—show unremitting growth. They also reflect the unceasing Soviet commitment to modernizing and expanding the USSR's Armed Forces.

The sustained Soviet economic commitment to the military is further revealed by the flow of resources to and growth of the machinery industry. This key sector of the economy, broadly divided into military and civilian machinery production, is the source of the Soviet Union's military hardware, civilian investment goods and consumer durables. The machinery sector continues to realize the most rapid growth in the economy, and in 1982, when overall industrial growth was 2.8 percent, the machinery sector expanded by five percent. The military machinery portion of

Weapons aboard the KIEV-Class carriers include, left to right, RBU-6000 ASW rocket launchers, SUW-N-1 long-range ASW rocket launchers, twin 76-mm dual purpose guns, four dual SS-N-12 surface-to-surface missile launchers, SA-N-3 surface-to-air missile launchers and 30-mm ADMG Gatling guns, seen beneath the bridge and on portside sponson.

tary has absorbed an increasing share of the nation's estimated gross national product (GNP). Even in a period of slowing economic growth, the Soviet military sector continues to maintain its priority claim on the nation's scarce economic resources.

Future Production

By any industrial or economic measure the Soviet Union has consistently made military materiel production its highest economic priority. The civil sector of industry has always been given a much lower priority in research, development and investment resulting in a poorer quality and quantity of product. Reports of industrial malaise and disruptions have primarily concerned the civilian sectors, although military industries have been slightly affected.

There has been considerable debate on whether the Soviets would change from high military production to more production for civilian consumption or remain committed to the intensive military-oriented philosophy for the rest of this decade and into the 1990s. The issue has centered on the economics of such a decision, and the premise that capital improvements need to be made in the basic industries, transportation and other nonmilitary sectors in order to achieve a balanced economy and thus higher economic and military potential. Historical evidence indicates that there probably will be no radical changes in Soviet industrial investment patterns and that the size of the military-related effort will remain substantial both in absolute terms and as a percent of the budget.

The Soviet commitment of resources to the military-industrial complex is large and growing. It is through the military that the Soviets have achieved a world power status. They will continue to produce the materiel necessary to maintain that status. There will be no slackening of the effort or resources committed to production for the Armed Forces.

this sector now accounts for 60 percent of total machinery output. The military portion of this all-important machinery sector has been receiving almost all the additions to the machinery sector's labor force, leaving little or no force growth for the civilian sector.

In current rubles, our best estimate of Soviet military spending, from 1970 through 1981, shows a significant increase at a rate faster than overall economic growth. As a result, throughout the last decade, the Soviet mili-

Chapter VI

Research and Development

The Soviet Union's military research and development (R&D) programs make a vital contribution to the continuing modernization and increased capabilities of the USSR's Armed Forces. In recent years, the USSR has significantly reduced the lead previously held by the United States and its Allies in technologies of military importance. The Soviet leadership gives military R&D high funding priority, with investment growing at a rate of six-to-seven percent a year. The continuing quest for improved technologies is reflected in the major military-related programs of Soviet research and development centers. Over the years this well-defined and highly capable defense R&D sector has evolved as essentially separate and distinct from the less capable civil sector.

Today, the Soviet Union has some 3,200 research institutes engaged in scientific and technical research, much of which is military or military-related. The major research, design and test facilities engaged in the development of Soviet military aircraft, missile and space systems have grown by at least 30 percent during the past 10 years. Key aerospace design bureaus have shown greater growth. For example, the Tupolev Design Bureau, responsible for the development of such aircraft as the new BLACKJACK strategic manned bomber, has doubled in size during the past decade. R&D centers and bureaus engaged in the development of ground and naval weapons systems have also continued to receive an increasing level of capital investment.

Concurrent with rising Soviet capital investment has been a significant growth in the

High-priority research and development are spurring the USSR's exploitation of space for military purposes. The Tyuratam Space Assembly and Launch Complex is being further modernized to support launchings of the Soviet space shuttle and new heavy-lift (upper right) and medium-lift (upper left) launch vehicles in the mid-to-late 1980s.

number of scientists and engineers in the USSR's military R&D program. Some 500,000 Soviet scientists and engineers are now graduating each year from an educational system strongly oriented toward science and technology. By contrast, in 1983, the United States graduated only 100,000 scientists and engineers. The Soviet Union's R&D force of more than 900,000 scientists and engineers is the largest in the world. Of this number, the best qualified are selected for military research and development.

The R&D Process

The development of Soviet weapons systems, from initial research to final production, involves a number of important participants, including:

- the research institutes of the Soviet Academy of Sciences,
- the defense industrial ministries,
- the design bureaus, where weapons development programs progress from the design concept to prototype and
- the weapons systems production and final assembly plants.

The political, industrial and scientific leaders associated with military R&D have generally enjoyed long tenure in their positions. This longevity has contributed to the high-level influence, stability, continuity and growth that have historically characterized the Soviet defense sector. The current Minister of Defense, D. F. Ustinov, serves as an excellent example. Placed in charge of Soviet weapons development and production during World War II, he has since enjoyed a succession of high-level positions in which he has been the central figure in Soviet military programs and the driving force behind the Soviet build-up over the past 25 years. He is a member of the Council of Ministers, the Defense Council and the Politburo. His long-term, central role provides the defense sector with a very influential voice in the Soviet political leadership.

The weapons development and acquisition process includes military R&D aimed at the incorporation of new technologies, paralleling continued use of proven technologies, long-term continuity of design teams and production leadership and multi-year funding.

In this process, the Ministry of Defense generates the weapons requirements, and design bureaus prepare the preliminary design for Party and government approval. Once this ap-

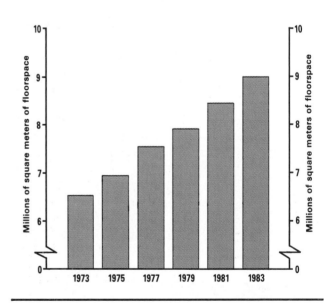

Key Soviet Research, Development and Test Centers

proval is given, multi-year funding is authorized for the entire design and development phase of each weapon system. No further funding decisions are necessary until the production phase.

Growth in Key Aerospace Research, Design and Test Facilities

Relative to their US counterparts, Soviet military planners are better able to marshal, focus and sustain the commitment and resources required for the development of new weapons systems. Weapons decisions at the level of the Politburo carry the force of law in the economy and are the rough equivalent of the United States combining a Defense Department program approval, a Presidential decision authorizing top priority for that program and multi-year Congressional funding. The result in the USSR is a continuing flow of increasingly capable weapons systems for the Soviet Armed Forces.

Key Technologies

Technological gains in Soviet weapons systems rely not only on the contributions of the indigenous R&D base but also on the acquisition of Western technology and its timely incorporation into Soviet weaponry. While the United States continues to lead the USSR in most basic technologies, the gap continues to narrow in the military application of such technologies. Increasingly, the incorporation of critical Western technologies is permitting the USSR to avoid costly R&D efforts and to produce, at a much earlier date than would otherwise be possible, Soviet weapons comparable to or superior to fielded US weapons.

Electronics: While still lagging in advanced technological achievements, the USSR is nearly equal to the West in electronics in deployed weapons systems. Advances in very large-scale integrated circuits and other advanced microelectronics are enabling the Soviets to process radar, acoustic sensor, laser and other signals faster, more accurately and more reliably than in the past. As a result, reaction times and accuracies of weapons can be significantly improved, and battlefield decisions can be rendered more quickly.

Computers: Because of past Soviet deficiencies in computer technology, computers were not included in their military systems to the extent found in Western systems. In recent years, however, such deficiences have been partially offset by indigenous advances and by the increased availability of Western computer equipment. Additionally, the Soviet R&D infrastructure has been reorganized to improve assimilation of Western computer advances, particularly for military applications.

Soviet advances in computer technologies will permit not only improvements in manufacturing capabilities and existing military systems but also the opportunity to explore entirely new applications. Artificial intelligence and robotics have a strong potential for military applications. Such technologies would enable the Soviets to develop highly sophisticated, unmanned weapons systems less vulnerable to the battlefield hazards of shock

and radiation. The Soviets are certain to examine the feasibility of these technologies during the 1980s, with potential weapons programs emerging in the 1990s.

Manufacturing Technologies: A major objective of Soviet R&D is to develop defense industry manufacturing technologies that can efficiently mass-produce the large number of weapons needed to support military goals. While the Soviet Union has excellent metalworking technologies such as casting, forging, extrusion, metal removal and welding, it continues to be plagued by problems in the production of critical items such as high-precision electrical and mechanical components and advanced microelectronics. Efforts to solve such problems are being assisted by the successful acquisition and assimilation of Western technology.

Structural Materials: The structural materials used in Soviet weapons systems have improved steadily since the 1950s. The US margin of technological superiority over the USSR in materials of military significance such as steels, aluminum alloys, titanium alloys, superalloys and advanced composites continues to diminish.

Over the past decade, the Soviet Union has established a large program to develop and apply advanced fiber-reinforced composites to military systems. The favorable strength-to-weight ratio of these polymeric and metal-alloy materials, as well as high-performance carbon and ceramic-based materials, makes advanced composites especially useful for high-performance aircraft and missile airframe applications.

Soviet construction of titanium-hulled submarines, which commenced in the mid-1950s, has been a formidable and costly engineering undertaking. By the early 1990s, the USSR will have several classes of titanium-hulled submarines. Such submarines have diving

ALFA-Class nuclear-powered attack submarine

depths significantly greater than steel-hulled submarines.

Directed Energy: The Soviets continue a major R&D effort aimed at the development of technologies applicable to directed energy weapons. Dating back to the mid-1960s, they have made a large, long-term commitment to the development of laser weapons. Their high-energy laser program, being conducted at numerous large, tightly guarded facilities, is considerably larger than the US program and continues to grow.

The Soviets are also pursuing technologies to support laser weapons development. This includes R&D on efficient electrical power sources and on the development of high-quality optical components. The USSR has developed a rocket-driven magnetohydrodynamic generator that produces 15 megawatts of short-term electric power, a generator that has no Western counterpart, which could provide a compact, light-weight power source for mobile or transportable laser weapons.

The Soviets also continue an intensive effort aimed at the development of high-power microwave and millimeter-wave sources for radio frequency weapons. Soviet radio frequency technology has now advanced to the stage where it could support development of a prototype, short-range radio-frequency weapon. Many Western weapons systems would be vulnerable to such a weapon, which not only could damage critical electronic components but also inflict disorientation or physical injury on personnel.

Finally, there is considerable research on the development of destructive particle-beam weapons. Such weapons could deliver intense energy particles at the speed of light, capable of penetrating the exterior of a target, destroying key internal components or igniting fuels and munitions. While much of the Soviet R&D effort in this field is on a par with that in the West, there are difficult technological problems to be solved. Technology to support development of such weapons is not expected to be available before the mid-1990s.

Propulsion and Propellants: Comprehensive propulsion and propellant research and development programs contribute to enhanced capabilities of all elements of the Armed Forces. The Soviets excel in the application of gas turbine engines for naval vessels. They are also developing advanced, unconventional marine propulsion systems for their submarines, which would be far quieter to reduce submarine detectability.

In aircraft and missile propulsion, the Soviets are drawing heavily on acquired Western technology to develop more advanced materials and production techniques. Several turbofan jet engine prototypes are in development that could significantly improve the performance of Soviet fighter and large transport aircraft. Some employ turbine cooling concepts even more advanced than those available in the United States. The Soviets have the technology to develop long-range supersonic ramjets for use in air-to-surface missiles, as well as in high-speed, low-altitude cruise missiles. Design programs have also begun on hypersonic ramjets, very high-speed propulsion systems with possible application in the Soviet reusable space vehicle program.

Solid- and liquid-fuel propellant R&D is very active. The Soviets continue to be world leaders in storable liquid propellant rocket engines and have deployed these engines in their large space launch vehicles, as well as in a number of the more recent ICBMs. They have pioneered in the use of rocket ramjets in sur-

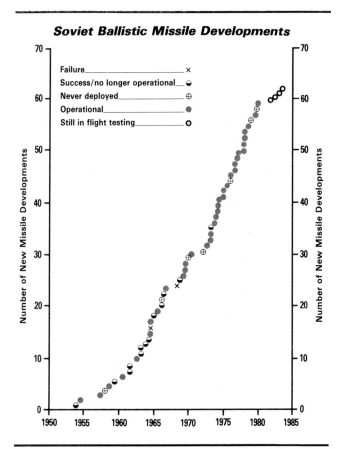

Soviet Ballistic Missile Developments

Failure _____ ×
Success/no longer operational __ ◕
Never deployed _____ ⊕
Operational _____ ●
Still in flight testing _____ ○

Number of New Missile Developments

YAK-36/FORGER VSTOL aircraft on the carrier MINSK.

face-to-air missiles. They are working on advanced rubber-base composite propellants, which have applications in defensive missile systems and for solid fueled ballistic missiles. Their ability to control propellant burning rates with chemical additives is on a par with that of the United States.

Explosives: In explosives R&D, the Soviets are upgrading their production capability for shaped-charge munitions. They lead the United States in enhancing fuel-air explosive effectiveness with metal powder overwraps and igniter coatings. These explosives advances contribute to the Soviet effort to improve substantially the battlefield effectiveness of their weapons against armored vehicles and troops.

Biological Research: The military applications of new biotechnology developments are also the subject of the R&D program, which is active in the development of militarily useful toxins and other physiologically active compounds with lethal or incapacitating effects. The Soviets are also performing genetic engineering research with applications not only for medicine, agriculture and industry but also for improving the effectiveness of disease-causing biological warfare agents.

Interest in improving the effectiveness of the personnel operating weapons systems is evident in a number of research programs. Research is also proceeding in the fields of pharmacology, neurochemistry and sensory physiology with the goal of finding drugs that will enhance the endurance and alertness of troops in the battlefield.

Technology Transfer

Acquisition of Western technology, essential to many Soviet technological advances, involves legal and illegal operations not only against the United States but also, increasingly, against other world technological leaders. The Soviets tend to regard Western system characteristics as a yardstick against which their technical capabilities must be judged. The Soviets are taking full advantage of opportunities afforded to acquire Western science and technology to strengthen both their military power and military-industrial base.

Soviet industrial modernization programs are supported by an elaborate network for the collection of foreign scientific and technological information. Guidelines for introduction of advanced manufacturing systems, including computer-aided design and automated manufacturing systems, include a constant monitoring of available Western technology.

No areas of Western technology are given higher priority than computers and electronics. KGB and GRU agents are targeted against Western sources for these critical technologies in order to determine exactly where and how the "hardware" and "software" can be acquired. Collection requirements are coordinated with the USSR weapons development and production system. Weapons designers and technologists submit their requests directly through the KGB departments located at each facility. The turnaround time for the desired information or "hardware" can be a matter of weeks. Standing S&T requirements are continually updated by the S&T elements of the KGB and GRU, as well as by the State Committee for Science and Technology, many of whose staff members are KGB and GRU officers. In addition, the USSR Academy of Sciences and several of its institutes follow Western S&T, even tapping into Western data bases through a growing number of transnational computerized networks dedicated to S&T collection and dissemination.

An analysis of nearly 800 cases involving Soviet acquisitions of Western technology has provided insight into the overall Soviet programs for obtaining militarily significant technology from the West and Japan. In these cases, over half the technologies acquired by the Soviets were either in electronics and computers or production and manufacturing equipment. Clandestine collection and embargo evasions accounted for many important Soviet acquisitions. However, while the illegal and covert technology collections have been important, it should be noted that the majority of Soviet acquisitions of Western technology have been achieved through legal means. Turnkey plants and legal purchases of process equipment with instructions are probably the most valuable long-term technology transfer mechanism, with their value largely dependent on the amount of instruction and training provided in the transaction.

Fresh evidence of such Soviet efforts to ac-

quire computer technology appeared early this year when German and Swedish officials seized approximately 50 tons of advanced US computers and integrated-circuit manufacturing technology with military applications that were being illegally diverted to the Soviet Union. This shipment had been routed through a half dozen Western countries underlining the extraordinary means the Soviets employ to bypass legal barriers and obliterate the trail of their collection program.

Virtually all major Soviet computer systems, such as the entire RYAD-series and the Soviet SM-series of minicomputers, are based on and reverse-engineered from Western computers acquired both legally and illegally. The Soviets have used and copied illegally acquired Western microelectronics such as microprocessors and have purchased Western technology and complete production plants for both integrated circuit and printed circuit-board production. More than one-third of all known Soviet integrated circuits have been copied from US designs. The acquisition of these militarily critical technologies has resulted in major reductions in the cost, time and risk involved in the Soviets' R&D effort. As a result, improvements have been made in performance capabilities of Soviet ground, naval and aerospace weapons. These improvements are now requiring the West to expand military development efforts in order to counter the increased Soviet threat.

Legal transfers of technology to the USSR have also been damaging to Western interests. The case of the shaped-charge warhead, first developed by the West during World War II for antitank munitions, offers a good example. After the war, the technology was transferred to the US oil tool and mining industry for use in perforating oil well casings, baring rock strata and for tapping blast furnaces. Over the years, universities, various industries and nondefense-related Government agencies acquired the technology. They studied the implosion process, improved the designs and published the results in open literature. The US literature was initially acquired by Soviet institutes involved in oil and mining research. From there, it was passed to the Soviet military R&D community, where it has since been exploited and played an important role in the development of Soviet munitions. In another case, a Hungarian scientist provided the Soviets with US magnetic bubble memory re-

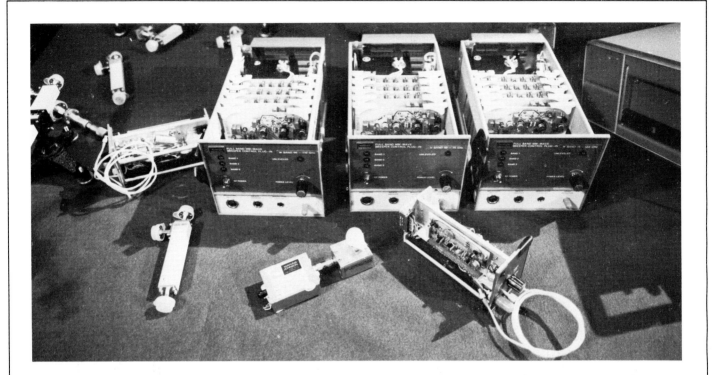

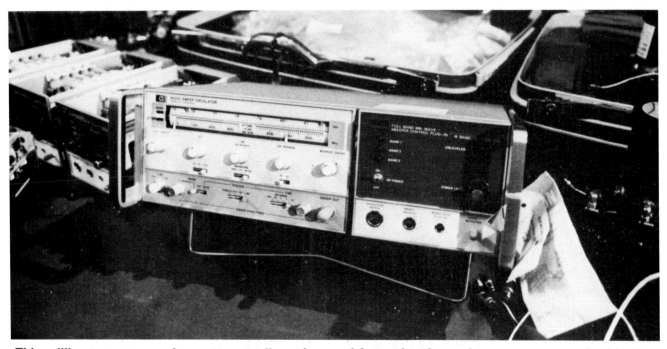

This millimeter-wave equipment, normally embargoed for national security reasons, was seized in the US enroute to the USSR as part of Operation Exodus in 1982. Covert acquisition of such key technologies by the USSR and its allies is a major objective of Soviet intelligence.

search information, of importance to advanced military computer developments. Under a US-funded grant, the scientist visited the United States and conducted research at a leading university. He also attended conferences and visited other facilities to observe and discuss US research. The scientist has ad-

mitted passing the information gained in the United States to the Soviets. The Hungarians claim and the Soviets admit that the Hungarian provided the Soviets their capabilities in magnetic bubble memory technology. One of the principal advances offered by magnetic bubble technology is the fact that it is a rug-

Chapter VI Research and Development

Soviet use of proven Western designs is evident in the An-72/COALER, a copy of the US Boeing YC-14 above and, facing page, the Il-76/CANDID, similar to the US Lockheed C-141 transport aircraft.

ged stable system that retains its "memory" even when power is off—an excellent candidate for military computer systems. This transfer advanced the Soviets by at least 10 years in an important emerging technology.

The Soviets have also made very effective use of the US-Soviet student exchange program. At least three-fourths of the Soviet students coming into the United States are in scientific and engineering fields, while their US counterparts are primarily in the social sciences and humanities. The Soviets who come to the United States under the graduate student and young faculty program generally already have the Soviet equivalent of a US PhD degree, average about 35 years of age and have 8 years of practical experience in their specialty. They are, without exception, capable scientists, many of whom are involved in military-related work in the USSR. The Soviet candidates have nearly always proposed research activities involving technologies that have direct military applications, and in which the Soviets are deficient. Knowledge gained in the West is returned to and retained in the Soviet Union.

Technology transfer can also clearly be seen in Soviet adaptation of Western aircraft structural designs. At a Paris Air show, the Soviets thoroughly examined the US C-141 jet transport. They photographed the aircraft, measured it and even took metal samples. The resulting structural similarities in a subsequent Soviet aircraft, the Il-76/CANDID, are quite striking. The performance characteristics of the Soviet Il-76/CANDID and the US C-141 are almost identical. In addition to its cargo role, the CANDID is being modified as an AWACs aircraft. In another such case, the pressing need of the Soviets for a transport aircraft with short-take-off-and-landing capability will be met by the An-72/COALER, a copy of the US Boeing YC-14. The similarity is the result of extensive and highly successful acquisition efforts carried out legally by the Soviets against US companies.

Achievements

With the continued growth of Soviet R&D and the high priority of defense R&D programs, technological breakthroughs could be achieved bringing Soviet advances in such

militarily critical areas as acoustic and non-acoustic anti-submarine warfare, missiles and space, directed-energy weapons and ballistic missile defense. Such breakthroughs could have a major impact on the military balance between the USSR and the United States.

The most important measure of the Soviet military R&D effort, the large capital and manpower investments, the technological advances and the acquisition and successful assimilation of Western technology, is that it has produced results for the USSR's Armed Forces. These results have been impressive both in terms of quality and quantity.

Since 1970, the Soviets have developed more than 20 new types of aircraft, 10 types of ballistic missiles, 25 types of aerodynamic missiles, over 50 new classes of naval ships, one third of which have been submarines, and at least 50 new ground force weapons. Equally large numbers of modifications have reached operational status. In qualitative terms, the aerospace, naval and ground force weapons continue to reflect a steady evolutionary progress that has brought significant improvement in the range, speed, accuracy and payload of major new Soviet weapons. Many of these systems are on a par with, or even in some cases exceed, the capabilities of Western weapons. For example, the new Soviet heavy-lift helicopter, the Mi-26/HALO, is twice the size of the largest US helicopter and has double the lift capacity of its Soviet predecessor. Significant Soviet improvements in fielded weapon systems continue to reduce and even close the qualitative gap that Western weapons have enjoyed in the past. By all indicators, this progress and the high priority placed on military R&D by the Soviet Union will continue through the 1980s and well into the 1990s. The net result of these efforts will be a steady flow of new, increasingly capable military weapons systems to the Soviet Armed Forces.

The Global Challenge

The Soviet Union's emergence as a global superpower has been based principally on its military capabilities. Although Soviet leaders regard military power as their primary strength in the international arena, they also view the East-West relationship as a more comprehensive struggle involving political, economic, social and ideological factors, which they characterize as "the correlation of forces." They profess confidence that this correlation is shifting in favor of socialism. Soviet policy has sought to shift this further through invasion, subversion, military and economic aid, the use of proxies, covert activities and political alignment with regimes or movements opposed to Western policies.

Despite declining Soviet economic performance and the increasing burden of defense spending, the USSR has continued to pursue a foreign policy that includes an aggressive expansion of Soviet influence abroad. Over the past decade, the USSR has become increasingly active in the Third World, reflecting Moscow's power projection capabilities and skillful exploitation of political developments. Avoiding direct military confrontation with the West, Soviet leaders have followed a cautious approach through the creation and exploitation of opportunities to enhance Soviet power and reduce Western influence.

The Soviets appreciate the influence of world opinion on public policy and attempt to manipulate it toward their own ends. World opinion, however, seldom keeps the Soviets

The CONDOR heavy-lift transport, estimated to join Soviet operational forces in 1987-88, will have triple the payload capacity of the Il-76/CANDID, be able to carry major weapons systems such as the SS-20 missile launcher, and provide a substantial increase in the Soviet Union's capabilities for military airlift worldwide.

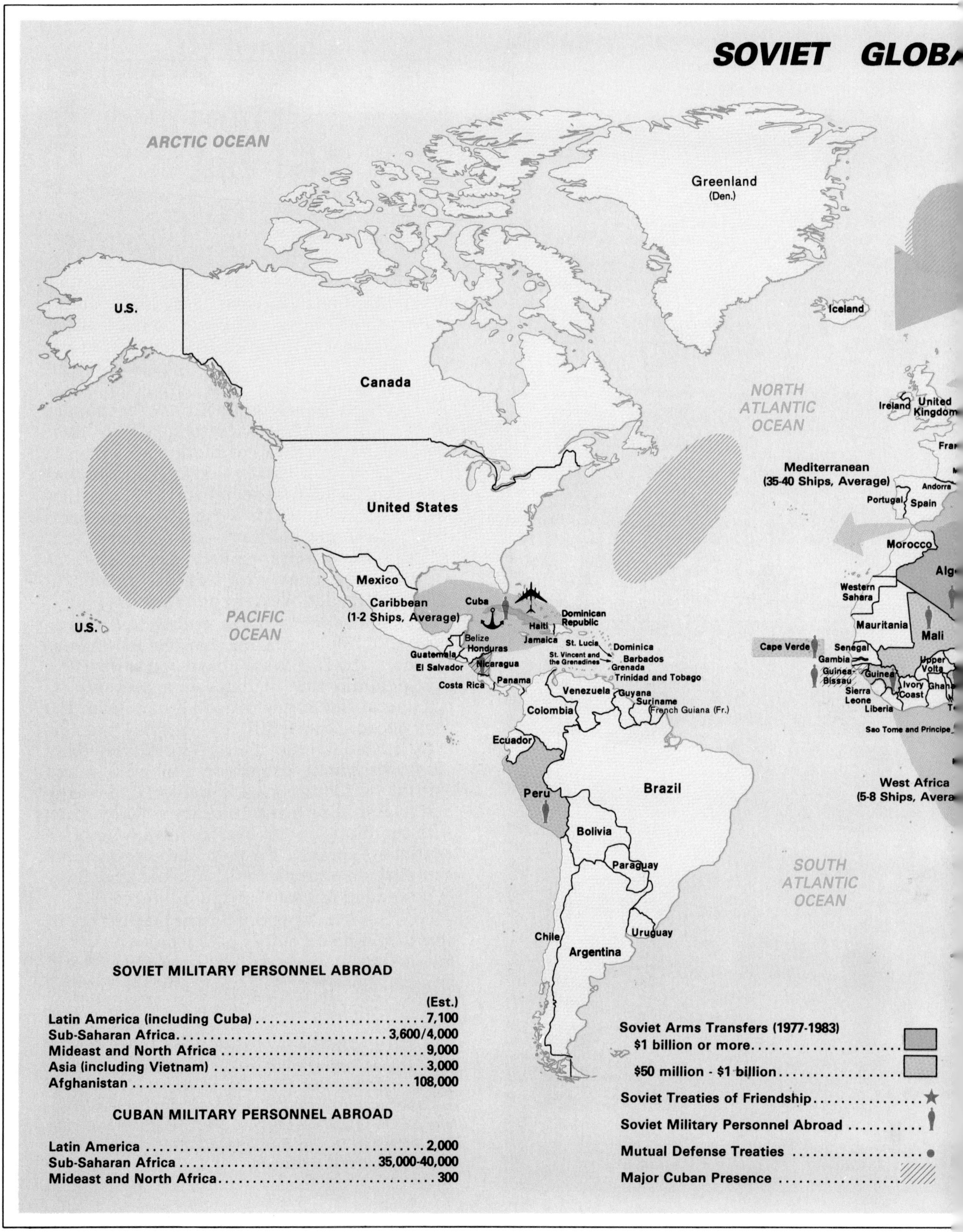

ARCTIC OCEAN

Greenland
(Den.)

U.S.

Canada

Iceland

NORTH
ATLANTIC
OCEAN

Ireland United
Kingdom

Mediterranean
(35-40 Ships, Average)

Fran

United States

Andorra
Portugal Spain

Morocco

Alg

Mexico

Western
Sahara

Caribbean
(1-2 Ships, Average)

Cuba

Dominican
Republic

Mauritania

Mali

U.S.

PACIFIC
OCEAN

Haiti
Jamaica

Belize
Honduras

St. Lucia

Dominica
Barbados
Grenada

Cape Verde

Senegal
Gambia
Guinea-
Bissau

Upper
Volta

Guinea

Ghana

Guatemala
El Salvador

Nicaragua

St. Vincent and
the Grenadines

Trinidad and Tobago

Sierra
Leone

Ivory
Coast

Costa Rica

Panama

Venezuela

Guyana
Suriname
(French Guiana (Fr.)

Liberia

Colombia

Sao Tome and Principe

Ecuador

Peru

Brazil

West Africa
(5-8 Ships, Avera

Bolivia

Paraguay

SOUTH
ATLANTIC
OCEAN

Chile

Uruguay

Argentina

SOVIET MILITARY PERSONNEL ABROAD

	(Est.)
Latin America (including Cuba)	7,100
Sub-Saharan Africa	3,600/4,000
Mideast and North Africa	9,000
Asia (including Vietnam)	3,000
Afghanistan	108,000

CUBAN MILITARY PERSONNEL ABROAD

Latin America	2,000
Sub-Saharan Africa	35,000-40,000
Mideast and North Africa	300

Soviet Arms Transfers (1977-1983)

$1 billion or more.....................

$50 million - $1 billion...............

Soviet Treaties of Friendship................ ★

Soviet Military Personnel Abroad ....

Mutual Defense Treaties .... ●

Major Cuban Presence ....

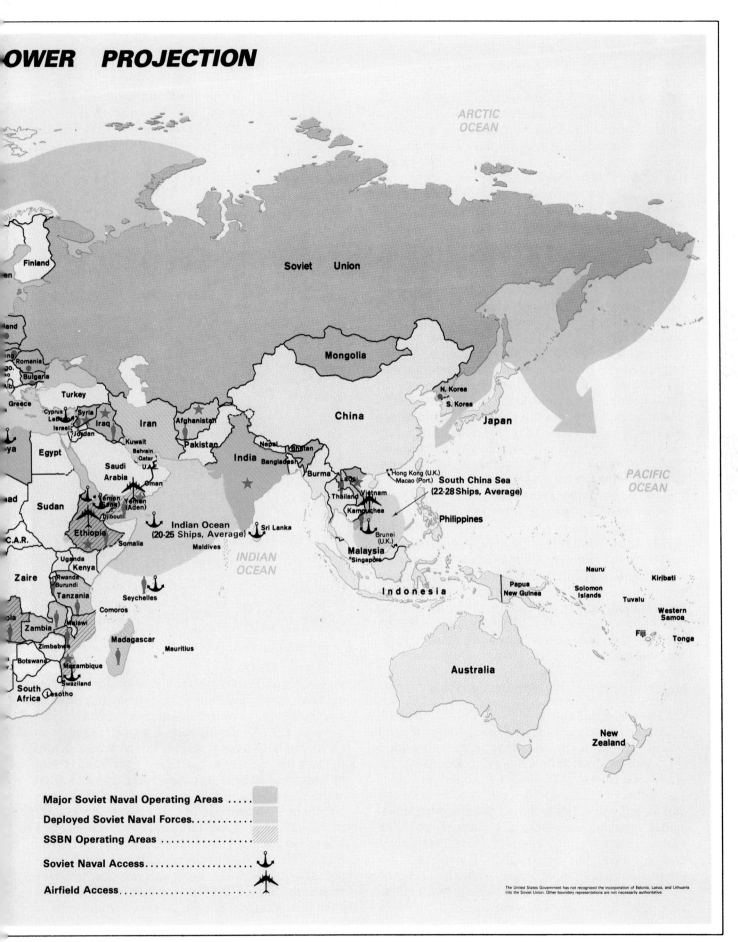

OWER PROJECTION

Major Soviet Naval Operating Areas .....

Deployed Soviet Naval Forces...........

SSBN Operating Areas ....

Soviet Naval Access...................

Airfield Access........................

The United States Government has not recognized the incorporation of Estonia, Latvia, and Lithuania into the Soviet Union. Other boundary representations are not necessarily authoritative.

from taking action in pursuit of their key national interests. The Soviets also have fewer domestic constraints on their foreign policy activities than Western nations. As Khrushchev's ouster would indicate, there is accountability within the Party for policies; however, public accountability is absent. There are no meaningful elections, free press or oversight committees. The highly structured nature of Soviet society permits the concentration of the nation's resources on the expansion of Soviet power and the manipulation of domestic opinion to legitimize policies.

Soviet foreign policy activities have never been merely reactive. The Soviet leadership looks upon competition and conflict as normal. Although Soviet global mobility forces have expanded and become more capable, they still do not match US capabilities.

Soviet policies are not constrained by a time imperative. Their deep sense of mission about the course of history imparts consistency of action over a long time, allowing them to make plans that do not have to produce immediate results. The Soviets have suffered many foreign policy setbacks. Nevertheless, they argue that reversals to their interests in international affairs are only temporary.

Besides military forces, the Soviets project power and influence through diplomacy, trade, aid, propaganda and covert activities. When these tools are used in a coordinated and skillful manner, Moscow can develop a web of influence in a target country and react rapidly to changing situations by applying the appropriate instruments. This technique allows the penetration of areas that may be beyond the immediate reach of Soviet military forces.

Instruments of Power Projection

Treaties of Friendship

Treaties provide a means whereby the USSR can advance its political and economic influence and establish a legal framework for closer relations with less-developed nations. The Soviet Union has 10 treaties of friendship and cooperation with Third World countries. These treaties vary slightly, but all call for mutual cooperation, respect for sovereignty and consultation on issues of common defense. Although none are mutual defense pacts such as those with East European countries and North Korea, with the exception of

the Congolese Pact, they have a general provision for military cooperation in the event of threats to peace and security. In Afghanistan, the Soviets justified invasion and occupation by reference to an alleged invitation from the Afghan government invoking the 1978 Soviet-Afghan Friendship Treaty. In Vietnam, the

Helicopter-tank operation in Afghanistan.

Soviet Treaty of Friendship, signed on 3 November 1978, provided Hanoi with political and military support against a possible Chinese attack. Vietnam felt it was necessary to have such a treaty prior to invading Kampuchea on 25 December 1978. This Treaty and subsequent events provided the Soviets with access to Vietnamese military facilities, particularly the complex at Cam Ranh. As events in the Middle East have shown, however, a friendship treaty is no guarantee that the Soviet Union will automatically support a co-signatory state. In the Iran-Iraq conflict, for example, the USSR has maintained relations with both countries despite the 1972 Treaty of

Friendship and Cooperation with Iraq. To the Soviets, treaties are manipulated in the manner most conducive to the interests of national policy objectives.

Arms Control Negotiations

The USSR's efforts to increase its global reach extend to the field of arms control negotiations. Arms control agreements contribute to shaping of the balance of military forces worldwide. Arms control negotiations provide an international forum that the Soviets attempt to use to their advantage.

While arms control agreements such as the 1968 Nuclear Non-Proliferation Treaty and the 1963 Hotline accord have made clear and important contributions to global security, other accords have made contributions that are less clear—particularly when the USSR has used such negotiations to seek advantage. The SALT process provides an important example. The USSR has stretched the limits and spirit of both the SALT I and SALT II Agreements in expanding and modernizing its strategic arsenal.

In addition, the Soviet Union has on occasion refused to accept effective verification procedures in some arms control agreements. The USSR would not permit its full European territory to be covered under the confidence-building measures in the 1975 Helsinki Final Act. For years, the Soviet Union has resisted a detailed examination in the Mutual and Balanced Force Reduction talks of the size and composition of its forces in Central Europe. It has resisted the introduction of adequate verification measures in an agreement barring chemical weapons and has worked to impede international investigation of chemical and toxin weapons use in Afghanistan, Kampuchea and Laos. Likewise, the Soviets have refused US proposals to negotiate essential verification improvements that would help assure the capability to monitor compliance with the Threshold Test Ban and the Peaceful Nuclear Explosion Treaties.

The Soviets have violated arms control agreements when they thought it would be in their interest. They have used, or supported the use of, chemical agents and toxin weapons in Afghanistan and Southeast Asia in violation of the Geneva Protocol and the Biological Weapons Convention. The Soviets have not in all instances complied with the Helsinki Final Act requirement of advance notification of certain major military exercises. They have violated the SALT II limits on encryption of missile test telemetry. A new large phased-array radar that they are now building in the central USSR is almost certainly in violation of the 1972 ABM Treaty. The SS-X-25 missile is probably a second new ICBM type, prohibited by the SALT II agreement; if it is not, it violates the SALT II provisions regarding the permitted ratio between the weight of an ICBM reentry vehicle and the missile's total throwweight. Although the data are somewhat ambiguous, it is likely that the Soviets have violated the Threshold Test Ban Treaty limits on the size of underground nuclear tests, and they may have deployed some SS-16 missiles in violation of SALT II. Other compliance concerns are being studied.

The Soviet record underscores the necessity of precise drafting and effective verification provisions in all future accords. But that alone will not be enough. Most fundamentally, the USSR must adopt a more responsible policy toward compliance. Furthermore, the traditional Soviet effort to achieve unilateral advantage through arms control treaties demonstrates that the West's determination to maintain a military balance is crucial to significant, equitable arms reductions. The Soviet Union will not have any incentive to accept such reductions unless it is convinced that the West will not allow it to achieve unilateral advantage within or outside the arms control framework.

Military Assistance

Military assistance is a major instrument of Soviet policy in the Third World. Today, 29 years after the Soviet arms sales program began with a $250 million agreement with Egypt, the USSR exports more arms and has more military technicians and advisers stationed abroad than any other country.

The Soviet Union's military assistance program includes arms sales and grants, military training, the deployment of military advisory groups and the use of proxy forces such as Cuban troops and East German intelligence and security personnel.

Moscow's military aid, besides being employed as an entree into regions previously beyond its influence, also has been used to foster dependency by assisting countries deficient in educational and technical assets. Frequently, the recipient of Soviet arms must

Major Soviet Equipment Delivered to the Third World 1978-1983

	Total	Near East and South Asia	Sub-Saharan Africa	Latin America	East Asia and Pacific
Tanks/Self-propelled Guns	7,390	5,245	1,080	305	760
Light Armor	10,040	7,910	1,650	175	305
Artillery	10,945	6,670	2,625	820	830
Major Surface Combatants	38	24	5	3	6
Minor Surface Combatants	150	19	42	34	55
Submarines	10	7	0	3	0
Missile Attack Boats	57	28	10	11	8
Supersonic Aircraft	2,465	1,745	250	165	305
Subsonic Aircraft	225	115	50	0	60
Helicopters	1,240	830	155	85	170
Other Combat Aircraft	395	130	80	70	115
Surface-to-Air Missiles	10,315	7,575	910	720	1,110

rely indefinitely upon the USSR for training and advisory support needed for the use and maintenance of sophisticated equipment.

Training: Training is designed to familiarize personnel with the operation and maintenance of Soviet equipment, doctrine, strategy and tactics. Some military personnel from pro-Soviet Marxist countries receive training as political officers, while others are trained in intelligence and internal security operations by KGB and GRU personnel. The training is conducted in the Soviet Union, Eastern Europe and in Third World countries by military advisers.

Arms Sales: From 1955-83, Moscow and its Eastern European Allies have signed contracts for $98 billion worth of military weapons and equipment to the Third World. A total of more than $60 billion had been delivered by the end of 1983. Arms deliveries by the USSR and the Warsaw Pact have been increasing very rapidly during the last decade. As a result of these rapid increases, the USSR and its Eastern European Allies overtook and surpassed total US sales and deliveries to the Third World in 1979. The Soviet military aid program is facilitated by the USSR's high level of arms production, variety of the weapons and equipment available and competitive prices and attractive financing. The USSR can meet customer needs often without denying equipment to its own forces. In addition, the USSR has exploited occasions when the West has been unwilling to supply sophisti-

cated arms to a region or particular country.

Since 1980, arms exports have kept a net profit in the USSR's trade with the Third World; military sales have accounted for as much as 60 percent of trade with developing countries. The acquisition of hard currency has been an increasingly important aspect of Soviet arms sales, in that hard currency payments from almost all of its buyers are now

Soviet Involvement in Africa

Diplomatic Relations with USSR (46)

Regular Naval Access

Regular Naval Air Access

Treaty of Friendship and Cooperation

	1964	1984
Military Advisers	545	6,500
Economic Advisers	2,400	22,000

required. In 1982, the Soviets earned over $6 billion in hard currency receipts from arms sales, and currently arms sales account for about 15 percent of their hard currency earnings.

Arms Agreements

The majority of exported Soviet weapons have gone to Arab countries in the Middle East and North Africa. Since 1955, these sales have accounted for nearly 60 percent of Soviet arms agreements to the Third World. Four other countries—India, Vietnam, Ethiopia and Cuba have accounted for more than 25 percent. Within the past decade the Soviets have also greatly expanded their arms deliveries in Latin America.

Middle East: Libya and Syria are the world's largest recipients of Soviet arms, with purchases of $15 billion and $13.8 billion, respectively, between 1954 and 1983. Since 1973, Moscow has been increasingly involved in providing support to the Syrian armed forces. Since the Lebanon conflict erupted again in 1982, the Soviets have virtually reequipped Syria. Newer and better equipment has been sent to Syria including the FLOGGER G aircraft. In addition, advanced SA-5 air defense missiles, currently manned by the Soviets, and SS-21 short-range ballistic missiles have been provided, the only deployment of such weaponry outside the Warsaw Pact. Libya maintains its ties with the Soviets as a result of its large arms purchase agreements. Soviet weaponry was used extensively during Libya's invasions of Chad. In 1981, the Soviet Union and Jordan embarked upon a limited arms relationship.

South Asia: In South Asia, India has been the major recipient of Soviet military assistance. Total military purchases from the Soviet Union in the period from 1954 through 1983 exceeded $10 billion, twice the value of arms India has purchased from the West. A $2.5 billion arms pact in 1980 and an additional $2.9 billion deal in 1982 were the largest arms agreements ever signed by India. The latest agreement includes the production, with Soviet collaboration, of T-72 tanks in India as well as of advanced model fighter aircraft, heavy transport aircraft, combat vehicles and a wide range of equipment for the Indian Navy, including submarines and missile-equipped frigates.

Southeast Asia: In Southeast Asia, the Soviet Union has used military aid as the primary means of gaining leverage in its relations with Vietnam. The December 1978 Vietnamese invasion of Kampuchea and the February 1979 Sino-Vietnamese border war resulted in massive Soviet arms deliveries to Vietnam, with lesser amounts going to Laos and Kampuchea. Soviet military assistance to Vietnam since 1979 has totaled more than $4.8 billion. Soviet equipment provided to Vietnam has included Su-22 swing-wing fighters, Mi-24 attack helicopters, missile attack boats, tanks and a variety of surface-to-air missiles. Soviet military assistance provided has enabled Vietnam to mobilize the world's third largest army—1.2 million troops—to maintain 150,000 to 180,000 troops in Kampuchea.

Southwest Asia: Historically, the USSR has sought to play a leading role in the affairs of Southwest Asia because of the region's proximity to the Soviet frontier. Growing Western military interests and dependence on Persian Gulf oil have further increased the importance of the region. Iraq has been a recipient of Soviet assistance since 1958 and ranks third among Moscow's arms recipients. The $3 billion in purchases in 1982 reflected replacements for Iraq's losses in the war with Iran. Prior to the February 1983 crackdown on the Soviet-backed Tudeh Communist Party and the subsequent expulsion in May 1983 of 18 Soviet diplomats, Moscow also had provided arms assistance to Iran, even during the Iran-Iraq War. On the Arabian Peninsula, the USSR and its East European Allies have been South Yemen's only arms suppliers for the past 5 years. Since 1967, Aden has signed at least $2.2 billion worth of arms agreements with Moscow.

Sub-Saharan Africa: Moscow is the dominant arms supplier to Sub-Saharan Africa. Ethiopia and Angola are the USSR's most important clients, with Ethiopia accounting for over 50 percent of all Soviet military sales to Sub-Saharan Africa since 1977. During the past 3 years, Moscow shipped an average of 25,000 metric tons of equipment worth about $1 billion to support Ethiopia militarily. In 1983, Moscow agreed to provide Angola with almost $800 million in military aid to support Luanda's fight against UNITA. The likelihood of continuing military conflict and instability in the Horn of Africa and Southern Africa provide the USSR with opportunities for continued sales in this region. Indeed, the Soviets recently have stepped up deliveries of sophisticated arms to Angola including air defense equipment and advanced jet aircraft.

Latin America: Since the early 1970s, the Soviets have used arms transfers to gain access and influence in Latin America. Massive Soviet economic and military aid has enabled Cuba to play an important role in the region and to maintain some 30,000 troops in Angola and Ethiopia. Since 1962, the USSR has shipped a yearly average of 34,000 metric tons of military equipment to Cuba. In 1983, as in 1982 and 1981, the Soviets far exceeded that average. While this program serves to modernize and expand

Cuba's military capabilities, it also allows for transshipment of weapons throughout the region, especially to Nicaragua and, until late 1983, to Grenada.

In 1983, arms deliveries by the Soviets and their allies to Cuba totaled over 50,000 metric tons. Major items delivered to the Cuban forces included:

• Air Force: at least seven MiG-21/FISHBED fighters, three MiG-23/FLOGGER fighters, two An-26/CURL transports, 16 Mi-17/HIP H helicopters, four Mi-14/HAZE and two Mi-2/HOPLITE helicopters.

• Air Defense Forces: at least 30 SA-3/GOA surface-to-air missile canisters, four SA-2/GUIDELINE missile transloaders, 11 ZSU-23-4 self-propelled anti-aircraft guns and eight electronic vans.

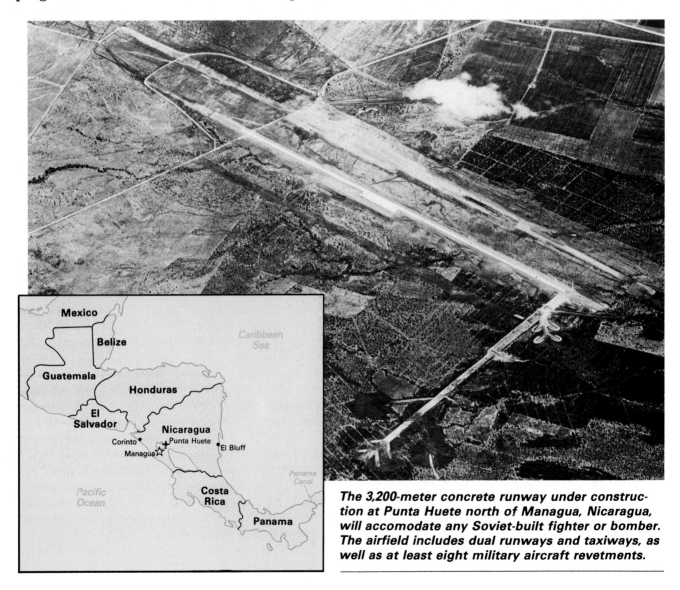

The 3,200-meter concrete runway under construction at Punta Huete north of Managua, Nicaragua, will accomodate any Soviet-built fighter or bomber. The airfield includes dual runways and taxiways, as well as at least eight military aircraft revetments.

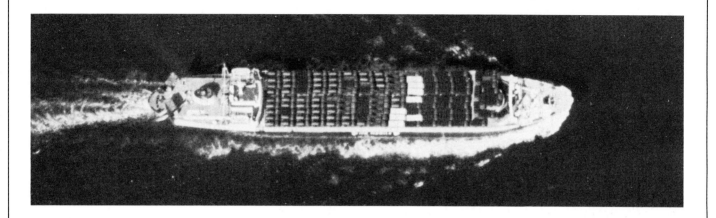

The Bulgarian-leased IFA MOBILE, at top, nears Corinto, Nicaragua, in July 1983 with a deck cargo of trucks and other wheeled equipment. The remote, guarded port of El Bluff, bottom, serves as the alternate point of entry for the Warsaw Pact's seaborne military deliveries.

• Naval Forces: at least three TURYA-Class PTH patrol hydrofoils and one 4,500-ton floating drydock.

• Ground Forces: at least 100 T-62 medium tanks, 11 BM-21 122-mm multiple rocket launchers, 83 ZIS-2 antitank guns, 51 130-mm field guns and four truck-mounted scissors bridges.

Cuban and Soviet military assistance to Nicaragua has been part of Moscow's effort to expand its influence in Central America. The USSR, its Warsaw Pact Allies and Cuba have made frequent arms deliveries to the Sandinistas to equip their 75,000 man armed forces structure. As was the case with Grenada, Cuba oversees the deliveries of military supplies to Nicaragua. In addition, Cuba maintains a 2,000 man advisory force in-country. Major items delivered to Nicaragua include:

• 44 T-55 tanks,

• 13 BTR-50 and BTR-60 armored personnel carriers,

• 20 BRDM armored reconnaissance vehicles,
• More than 150 howitzers, anti-tank guns, mortars, rocket-propelled grenade launchers,
• 8 transport aircraft (An-2/COLT, An-26/CURL),
• 14-18 helicopters (Mi-2/HOPLITE and Mi-8/HIP),
• 120 air defense artillery guns,
• 30 SA-7/GRAIL surface-to-air missiles, and
• thousands of infantry weapons.

Nicaragua claims the equipment being delivered is for agricultural and economic purposes, but unusually tight security measures are followed when ships are unloaded at the Pacific port of Corinto. Moreover, clandestine arms deliveries have been made to the smaller port of El Bluff on the Caribbean.

Beginning in March 1973 with a $200 million contract for ground force equipment, Moscow embarked on a comprehensive arms sales program to Peru. To date, Peruvian purchases have totaled $1.6 billion.

In contrast, US policy in Central America has not encouraged an arms race and continues to seek stability in the area. Armament levels were conspicuously low throughout Central America until Cuba and the Soviet Union began introducing large quantities of arms into Nicaragua. Since 1981, the USSR and Warsaw Pact allies have delivered nearly 17,500 tons of military equipment to Nicaragua.

Soviet Military Advisers

Moscow has increased its influence in the Third World through the presence of over 21,000 military advisers and technicians in nearly 30 countries. An additional 120,000 Soviet troops are stationed in Afghanistan, Cuba and Syria. The functions of these advisers and technicians include the training of the local military in maintenance and tactics, organizing and staffing military schools and high-level military staffs, constructing military facilities and, in a few instances, even providing combat support for indigenous troops. The result is that the Soviets are able to cultivate pro-Soviet sentiments, influence local military policies and infuse Communist ideology. The number of Soviet advisers and technicians abroad has increased nearly seven-fold since 1965.

The presence of advisers, in addition to assisting Third World military and security forces to improve their capabilities, increases the client state's dependence upon Moscow, improves Soviet intelligence collection, permits direct involvement in internal affairs and furthers Soviet access to facilities to enhance military power projection worldwide.

There are about 9,000 advisers stationed in the Middle East and North Africa. The increasing quantity and sophistication of military equipment supplied to Syria and Libya have led to a greater dependence on the Soviets for training, logistical and technical assistance as well as advisory support during actual operations.

In 1980, the number of Soviet military advisers assisting the 25,500-man South Yemeni Armed Forces increased to about 750. Most of the advisers serve in training, maintenance and logistics roles, although an undetermined number of the new advisers are reportedly assigned to artillery battalions and to the military academy in the capital.

The Soviet Union also maintains a 750-man military advisory mission in North Yemen. Soviet advisers are attached to all services but are most heavily involved in maintenance and training programs for the largely Soviet-equipped army and air force.

Between 100 and 200 Soviet military advisers may still be working in Iran despite a worsening of relations. Conversely, there are more than 450 Soviet military advisers working in Iraq. Soviet-Iraqi relations have not been smooth, but Iraq remains dependent on Moscow for much of its military equipment.

Over 3,500 Soviet military advisers in Sub-Saharan Africa are concentrated mainly in Ethiopia and Angola. Those in Ethiopia, some 1,700 in number, have been particularly active in advising the armed forces engaged in counterinsurgency operations against Tigrean and Eritrean insurgents. They also run the Soviet naval facility in the Dahlak Archipelago.

Moscow has 200 technicians in India to assist the Indian Armed Forces and defense industry in the maintenance and co-production of Soviet equipment. The largest concentration of Soviet military advisers in Asia is in Communist Indochina. Vietnam hosts 2,500 and Laos 500. These are predominantly technical personnel who conduct training and maintain Soviet-supplied equipment.

In Latin America, the Soviet Union has military advisers in Peru and Nicaragua. In Cuba, 2,800 Soviet military advisers are attached to military schools and to units with sophisticated equipment such as MiG aircraft, surface-to-air missiles and modern naval combatants. These Soviet advisers also supervise major military construction projects. In addition to some 6,000 to 8,000 civilian advisers, the Soviets have about 2,000 personnel attached to a signals intelligence facility and 2,600 military personnel in a motorized rifle brigade.

In Nicaragua, the Soviets have continued to rely mostly on the Cubans to provide overt assistance. Approximately 100 Soviet military and security personnel in that country are attached to the Sandinista military hierarchy, providing intelligence support and assistance in military planning and organization.

Soviet Proxies

Moscow has been able to enlist the assistance of its Allies as surrogates in situations where it normally would not have easy access or where its participation might be counterproductive to its objectives. The use of proxies permits the promotion of anti-Western causes and the extension of Communist influence while minimizing Moscow's risk. Proxy forces are intended to project the appearance of international support to "progressive" forces in a regional conflict.

Some 40,000 Cuban troops and advisers are active throughout Africa and the Middle East. Soviet-sponsored Cuban troops and advisers are active in the Caribbean and Central America. Additionally, nearly 3,000 East Europeans in the Third World train police and security cadres and intelligence operatives, penetrating local governments and developing pro-Moscow local Communist parties and front organizations.

Among Moscow's proxies, Cuba is undoubtedly the most important. The Castro regime is totally dependent upon Moscow's military, economic and political support. Military support to Cuba in the last 3 years is valued at over $1.7 billion. In addition, Moscow has been willing to underwrite Cuba's economy at a cost of $12 billion between 1981-83.

Cuba's active duty military and paramilitary forces are larger than those of Canada, Brazil or Mexico. With Soviet assistance Cuban military forces have grown to over 25 divisions, 950 tanks, over 270 jet combat air-

craft, 208 surface-to-air missile launchers, three submarines, two frigates, and over 50 armed patrol naval combatants.

Since 1980, Cuba has been creating a huge territorial militia. In a speech in July 1983, Castro claimed that "more than 500,000 men and women and tens of thousands of officers were organized into the militia, trained and armed in less than a year ... 1.8 million Cuban women have made the decision to volunteer to join the militia ... In the next 12 months, 500,000 other men and women and 30,000 new officers will join the militia ... One million additional combatants will join the Armed Forces and reserves." Once these goals are reached, the Cuban militia and reserves will be larger than the US National Guard and Reserves combined. When complete, Castro's militia program will make Cuba one of the most militarized nations in the world, with about two of every nine Cuban citizens having received military or paramilitary training. The large militia will free Cuban active duty forces for deployment elsewhere in the world as Soviet proxies.

Today, Moscow has been able to foment instabilities in Central America and remain largely shielded from accusations of being a source and abettor of political violence by using Cuba.

Approximately 6,000 Cuban civilians in Nicaragua are providing advice at many levels of government, including public health, education, construction and the Nicaraguan intelligence and security services. About 2,000 Cuban military advisers are with Nicaraguan armed forces.

Cuba's increased power projection capabilities in the Western Hemisphere were demonstrated last May when Cuban forces conducted several amphibious training exercises involving Cuba's two POLNOCNY-Class medium landing ships and other elements of the Cuban Navy. These were the first observed integrated amphibious exercises using the recently-supplied Soviet-built landing ships and the Cuban naval infantry. Even though small in scope, these exercises showed Cuba's growing ability to undertake amphibious assaults, especially in the Eastern Caribbean area where many of Cuba's island neighbors have little or no armed forces of their own.

Cuba's ability to carry out operations at great distances from its shores and serve Soviet objectives was demonstrated in Syria following the outbreak of the October 1973 war in the Middle East, in Angola in 1975-76 and in Ethiopia in 1978.

In Angola, 25,000 Cuban combat troops support the MPLA in its efforts to neutralize the National Union for the Total Liberation of Angola, UNITA. Another 6,000 to 7,000 Cuban civilian advisers and technicians provide vital support to the Angolan civil infrastructure.

About two-thirds of the non-Soviet Warsaw Pact military advisers in the Third World are East Germans who concentrate on intelligence and security training. East Germans have worked closely with intelligence and security organizations in South Yemen, Libya, Angola, Ethiopia, Ghana and Mozambique, and to a lesser degree in Afghanistan, Zambia, Tanzania and probably Vietnam.

There is also increasing evidence that the USSR directly trains or supports terrorists worldwide in order to achieve Soviet goals, while avoiding direct confrontation with the West. An example of the development of Soviet involvement with a terrorist group may be seen by examining Soviet support for the PLO. Originally, its pro-Arab, anti-Western, radical activities served Soviet purposes so well that the PLO received aid ranging from provision of arms and training to support for PLO recognition by the United Nations. Moscow was able to achieve a mutually beneficial arrangement with the PLO; in return for Soviet backing of its efforts in the Middle East, the PLO supported revolutionary activities directed against several Latin American governments. In late 1980, PLO Chairman Arafat revealed that he had offered Cuba the cooperation of the Palestinian resistance in support of the Latin American ''revolution.''

Access to Overseas Facilities

Soviet military assistance relationships with countries of the Third World frequently develop to the stage where the USSR is granted military overflight privileges, servicing agreements for Soviet aircraft and ships and military access to facilities. This access has enhanced the ability of Soviet air and naval forces to conduct prolonged operations in distant areas. Thus, military access to facilities in Vietnam, Syria, Ethiopia, South Yemen, Angola and Cuba has reduced the Soviet need for a larger number of ships in transit to maintain a naval presence.

Access to facilities for Soviet naval combatants, auxiliaries and aircraft ranges from occasional port visits, berthside restocking and minor maintenance and use of local shipyards for overhaul, to the right to construct and operate installations for logistics and ordnance storage. Generally, Moscow has succeeded in gaining military access in countries where the local regime needed military support.

The current Soviet philosophy that facilities should supplement, but not replace, support afloat, affects the amount of monetary investment Moscow is now willing to make in a foreign facility. The USSR spent substantial sums developing exclusive facilities at the port of Alexandria and Cairo West airfield in Egypt, and Berbera in Somalia, only to lose them when it was expelled from both coun-

Primary Soviet Submarine Deployment Areas 1964

Includes all operational
Soviet submarines

Primary Soviet Submarine Deployment Areas 1984

Includes all operational
Soviet submarines

Tu-16/BADGER strike and electronic combat aircraft are now with Soviet Forces at Cam Ranh, Vietnam.

tries in 1973 and 1977, respectively. Based on that experience, the Soviets recently have attempted to minimize their capital investment in overseas facilities. For example, the Soviets have used easily movable equipment at Dahlak Island, Ethiopia, or used previously developed local assets at Cam Ranh Bay, Vietnam.

Soviet reliance on overseas facilities is heaviest in the case of air operations, enabling long-range aircraft to conduct military airlifts and reconnaissance over large parts of the world not reachable from Soviet territory. The five-fold increase in naval air deployments since 1979 indicates that aircraft are an important component of the Soviet Ocean Surveillance System, which also includes satellites and merchant and fishing ships.

In Indochina, Moscow has established a major military presence centered on the former US naval facilities at Cam Ranh Bay, Vietnam. Exclusive access to Cam Ranh permits the Soviet Navy to operate in Southeast Asia on a continuing basis and to deploy to the Indian Ocean in a crisis. Cam Ranh provides major support to the Soviet naval presence of some 20 to 25 ships in the South China Sea. Soviet naval reconnaissance, strike and ASW aircraft are now deployed to Cam Ranh. Using this facility permits ongoing intelligence collection and ASW missions against US naval units operating in or transiting the South China Sea, activities near the US naval base at Subic Bay in the Philippines, and against PRC naval forces and installations on Hainan Island and the southern coast of China as far north as Hong Kong.

The Soviets have routine access to naval and air facilities in South Yemen. Since 1978, reconnaissance aircraft have flown patrols from Aden International Airport against US and Western naval ships in the Indian Ocean and the Arabian Sea. Improvements are being made at Aden International, including the extension of the runway to 3,500 meters. If long-range TU-95 BEAR D reconnaissance aircraft were deployed to Aden, the Soviets could extend their coverage of the region as far south as Diego Garcia.

The Soviet Indian Ocean Squadron uses its exclusive facilities in Ethiopia's Dahlak Archipelago in the Red Sea as its primary source of logistics and maintenance support. Ship visits have averaged about 70 per year for the past 5 years. Since April 1983, ships of the Soviet Mediterranean fleet have also called at Dahlak for maintenance and repairs. The most valuable piece of equipment there is an

8,500-ton floating drydock, which services both Soviet and Ethiopian vessels.

Soviet naval ships operating in the South Atlantic use Luanda, Angola as their primary logistics and maintenance base. The West Africa patrol has the mission of maintaining a Soviet presence and providing a contingency show of force. In wartime, it could threaten sea lines of communication. During the Falkland Islands conflict in 1982, Tu-95s from Luanda conducted limited surveillance of British naval forces en route to Ascension Island.

The heavy reliance of Libya on Soviet equipment and advisers has made Qadhafi more amenable to increasing Soviet access. Since 1981, ships from the Soviet Mediterranean Squadron have made port visits to Tripoli and Tobruk. Soviet Il-38/MAYs have made reconnaissance flights over the Mediterranean and conducted training exercises with Soviet combatants.

Since 1969, Soviet Navy task groups have made 21 deployments to Cuba, with port calls at Havana and Cienfuegos, and have conducted operational transits of the Gulf of Mexico. Approximately half of these deployments have included one or two submarines. The task groups have spent an average of 40 days in the Caribbean; the longest deployment of 91 days was in 1978.

Naval air deployments to Cuba began in 1970 and, since November 1981, the Soviets have used Cuba's San Antonio de los Baños military airfield as a permanent facility for maritime reconnaissance deployments of Tu-95 BEAR Ds and, since early 1983, Tu-142 BEAR Fs. Previously, joint missions by deployed BEAR Ds (reconnaissance aircraft) and BEAR Fs (ASW aircraft) had only been flown by Soviet aircraft based in Vietnam. BEAR F deployments could represent an increase in Soviet attempts to track US ballistic missile submarines deploying from East Coast ports. The Soviet signals intelligence complex near Havana has grown by 60 percent since 1970 and is the most extensive Soviet facility of this type outside the USSR. The importance of the facility is that it provides the Soviets, together with similar facilities in the USSR, complete coverage of the global beams of all US geosynchronous communications satellites.

Soviet intelligence collection operations from Cuba are supplemented by Cuban opera-

tions using Soviet-supplied equipment. In 1983, evidence was received that Soviet signals intelligence equipment had been mounted on a Cuban merchant ship, the ISLA DE LA JUVENTUD. This equipment will enhance the Cubans' capability to collect intelligence within the Caribbean area against the United States as well as their Caribbean neighbors.

Economic Aid

The Soviet Union's economic aid program is well below the funding allocated to arms aid. As a result of aid to Angola, economic aid for 1982 rose to about $880 million after a 5-year low of $521 million recorded in 1981.

The character of the Soviet economic aid program provides some insight into the criteria followed by the USSR for disbursement of funds. The bulk of economic aid agreements are with pro-Soviet Marxist governments; Angola, Cuba, Ethiopia, Afghanistan, Nicaragua and Vietnam continue to be major recipients of the Soviet aid program.

The USSR also pursues its economic aims through agreements designed to expand Soviet markets for equipment, balance trade and earn hard currency or equivalent goods. Multimillion dollar agreements to sell equipment on deferred terms to Argentina, Brazil, Greece, India, Iran, Mozambique, Nicaragua, Pakistan and Syria were under study at the end of 1983.

The agreements under negotiation will increase the commercial emphasis of the Soviet aid program. Historically, the USSR has almost exclusively used bilateral agreements for disbursement of its economic aid rather than going through international organizations such as the United Nations. Bilateral agreements give the Soviets more flexibility in dictating terms and utilizing such agreements in support of overall policy objectives.

By contrast, US economic assistance is the largest of any nation. In 1982, US bilateral assistance in grants and loans totalled over $8.1 billion in addition to an annual $750 million contribution to the International Development Agency, the concessionary financing organization of the World Bank. The United States agreed in 1981 to purchase $8.8 billion in shares to increase the general fund of the World Bank. Moreover, the United States in 1983 committed itself to contribute $8.4 billion to the International Monetary Fund (IMF). The resulting increase in resources will allow the IMF to help nations weather balance of payments crises. As a result of both the larger size of the US contribution and its distribution through international institutions, US contributions to economic development are dispersed throughout the world. In contrast, the Soviet program is concentrated in a small number of countries.

Espionage

The Soviets have continued to place emphasis on clandestine activities focused primarily on the acquisition of scientific and technological data in the United States, Western Europe and Japan. Blatant illegal activities by Soviet officials, largely in pursuit of such information, have resulted in a substantial increase over the past year of expulsions of Soviet personnel abroad.

In 1983, it was publicly revealed that some 135 Soviet diplomats and commercial personnel voluntarily left or were expelled from 19 countries as a result of charges of espionage and engaging in illegal activities. The largest numbers of expulsions were 47 from France in early April and 18 from Iran in mid-May. Soviet expulsions in 1983 represented a substantial increase over the past 3 years: 116 in 1980, 27 in 1981 and 49 in 1982.

Industrial and military espionage was the common thread running through most of these expulsion cases. Japan expelled two Soviets in June for attempts to steal computer technology and set up a spy ring in a Japanese computer company. In September, Ireland accused the Soviets of contacts with Irish terrorist groups and of using Ireland as a base for spying on the United Kingdom. Subsequently, two Soviet diplomats were expelled.

The expulsion from France of 47 diplomats,

BAL'ZAM-Class intelligence collection ships monitor US strategic and general purpose forces.

Chapter VII The Global Challenge

journalists and international civil servants probably had the greatest impact on Soviet espionage activities. Paris accused the USSR of organizing an extensive spy network involved in the collection of military-related scientific and technological information.

Case Studies in Military Power

Soviet reliance on the military to achieve national security objectives has been evident worldwide. The following case studies provide an insight into the different dimensions of the USSR's application of military influence and power.

Grenada

Events in Grenada between March 1979 and October 1983 demonstrate the techniques employed by the Soviets and their Cuban proxies to assist a radical leftist party in maintaining power and to use that party to further their own objectives. Grenada was an important part of a larger Soviet effort to change the political alignment in the Caribbean basin and to improve its own strategic position in the region vis-a-vis the United States.

The extent of Soviet and Grenadian relations after the March 1979 coup by Maurice Bishop was not generally publicized. Agreements were signed by the two states, but were kept secret and executed largely by Cuba as the intermediary. Soviet military and economic aid to Grenada was funneled through Cuba, which provided a wide range of economic, technical and military assistance. Havana granted at least $30 million toward the construction of the Point Salines airport and established a Cuban military mission in Grenada to assist in organizing and training the Grenadian military forces. By October 25, 1983, Grenada had 1,000 men under arms and more military supplies than all of its East Caribbean neighbors combined.

The extent of Soviet penetration of the island was revealed in documents found by the United States and other members of the Caribbean Multinational Force in October 1983. These documents show that in October 1980 Moscow secretly signed the first of four agreements to provide free military aid and training to Grenada. This agreement provided materiel worth over $6 million to be delivered to Cuba and then transshipped to Grenada. Similar Soviet agreements in February 1981

and July 1982 granted the Grenadians additional military equipment worth $31 million.

From Cuba the Maurice Bishop government received over 3,400 Soviet rifles, 200 machineguns, 100 pistols, 100 shoulder-fired rocket launchers, mortars, cannons and anti-aircraft guns in April 1979. These 3,800 infantry weapons and millions of rounds of ammunition arrived long before the new government had set up a formal military establishment. The Soviet Union quickly moved to bolster the regime with promised deliveries of large quantities of additional weapons. The following is a list of weapons uncovered during the multilateral action in October, 1983:
- over 9,000 rifles and machineguns,
- over 40 crew-served weapons,
- over 5,000,000 rounds of ammunition, and
- vehicles and miscellaneous military equipment.

On-scene observers indicated that this quantity of arms and equipment was sufficient to equip two Cuban infantry battalions for 30 to 45 days of combat.

The Soviets and Cubans in return were to receive benefits such as access to the Point Salines airport, then under construction by the Cubans. The Soviets were also studying the feasibility of developing a sea port to which they would have free access. The Soviets, with East German assistance, were in the process of improving the telecommunications links on the island by installing a satellite station and the modernization of Grenada's telephone system. Additionally, Bulgaria and North Korea were providing assistance to Grenada.

A large percentage of US sea trade and 40 percent of oil imports pass through the Caribbean. Strategic planning for the US Navy requires free movement of ships from ports on the Gulf of Mexico and through the Panama Canal, a vital sealane chokepoint. With a fully operational 3,000 meter runway on Grenada under Cuban/Soviet control, MiG-23s from Cuba and Grenada would have been able to interdict the Caribbean sea lanes. Use of the Grenada runway would have allowed flights from Europe and the Middle East into Central America to avoid landing in territory not controlled by the Soviet Union and its surrogates. For example, the Libyan airplanes detained in Brazil in April 1983 for clandestinely ferrying a cargo of military supplies to Nicaragua

POL Storage Area

New Cuban
Housing Area

Hardy Bay

Medical School

Construction of Point Salines Airfield, Grenada, in early 1983.

Chapter VII The Global Challenge

AGREEMENT

between the Government of Grenada and the
Government of the Union of Soviet Socialist Republics on deliveries from
the Union of SSR to Grenada of special
and other equipment

The Government of Grenada and the Government of the Union
of Soviet Socialist Republics,

guided by aspirations for developing and strengthening
friendly relations between both countries on the principles of
equality, mutual respect of sovereignty and non-interference into internal affairs,

proceeding from the desire to promote strengthening the independence of Grenada

and in connection with the request of the Government of
Grenada

have agreed upon the following:

Article 1

The Government of the Union of Soviet Socialist Republics
shall ensure in 1982-1985 free of charge the delivery to the
Government of Grenada of special and civil equipment in nomen-
clature and quantity according to Annexes 1 and 2 to the present
Agreement to the amount of 10.000.000 Roubles.

Article 2

The delivery of the equipment listed in Annexes 1 and 2 to the
present Agreement shall be effected by the Soviet Party by sea,
at the port of the Republic of Cuba.

The order of the further delivery of the above equipment
from the Republic of Cuba shall be agreed upon between the Grenadian and Cuban Parties.

Article 3

The Government of the Union of SSR at the request of the
Government of Grenada shall ensure rendering technical assistance in mastering of the equipment under delivery by receiving in
the USSR Grenadian servicemen for training in the operation,
use and maintenance of the special equipment as well as by sending
Soviet specialists to Grenada for these purposes.

The Grenadian servicemen shall be sent to the USSR for
training without their families.

The expenses connected with the Grenadian servicemen's training, upkeep, meals in the Soviet military educational establish-
ments as well as with their travel fare from Grenada to the USSR
and back shall be borne by the Soviet Party.

The Government of Grenada shall provide at its own expense
the Soviet specialists and interpreters with comfortable fur-
nished living accommodation with all the municipal utilities,
medical service and transport facilities for the execution of
their duties and shall ensure their having meals at reasonable
prices at the places of their residence.

The Soviet specialists and interpreters shall not be impo-
sed by any taxes and duties on entering or leaving Grenada and
during their stay there. All other expenses connected with deputation of the Soviet specialists to Grenada shall be borne by
the Soviet Party.

Article 4

The Soviet Party in periods to be agreed upon between the
Parties shall depute a group of Soviet specialists to Grenada to
determine expediency, opportunity and scope of rendering technical assistance in the creation of the stationary shop for repair
of the special equipment and transport, commanding staff trainer
school, training facilities for Armed Forces as well as the deliveries of missing building materials for construction of the sto-
rehouses and road.

The deputation of a group of Soviet specialists shall be effected on the terms and conditions of Article 3 of the present
Agreement.

Article 5

The Government of the Union of SSR shall ensure free of
charge the transfer to the Government of Grenada of necessary
technical descriptions, instructions and manuals in standard
composition on operation of the special equipment delivered under the present Agreement.

Article 6

The appropriate Grenadian and Soviet organizations shall
conclude contracts in which there shall be stipulated the detailed terms and conditions of deputing Soviet specialists, receiving for training Grenadian servicemen and other services connected with the implementation of the present Agreement.

Article 7

The Government of Grenada shall not without the consent of
the Government of the Union of Soviet Socialist Republics sell
or transfer, formally or actually, the special equipment, delivered under the present Agreement, the relevant documentation
and information or give permission to use the equipment and documentation by a third party or any physical or legal persons
but the officials and specialists of the citizenship of Grenada
being in the service with the Government of Grenada.

The Government of the Union of SSR and the Government of
Grenada shall take all the necessary measures to ensure keeping
in secret the terms and conditions of the deliveries, all the
correspondence and information connected with the implementation
of the present Agreement.

Article 8

The present Agreement comes into force on the date it is
signed on.

Annexes 1 and 2 are an integral part of the present Agreement.

Done in Moscow on July   " 27 ", 1982 in two origi-
nals, each in the English and Russian languages, both texts being
equally valid.

FOR AND ON BEHALF   FOR AND ON BEHALF

OF THE GOVERNMENT OF GRENADA   OF THE GOVERNMENT OF THE UNION
                                OF SOVIET SOCIALIST REPUBLICS

During the Soviet and Cuban penetration of Grenada from 1979-1983, secret agreements such as the Soviet-Grenadian military aid and training agreement, at left, involved at least $37 million of arms.

could have carried out their mission with impunity by using the Grenadian airport as a stopover point.

As a result of Soviet and Cuban activities, the threat to Grenada's neighbors was immediate and direct. The Organization of Eastern Caribbean States (OECS) statement of October 25, 1983, noted that "the extensive military buildup on Grenada over the past few years has created a situation of disproportionate military strength between Grenada and other OECS countries." Already concerned by Grenada's activities as a training ground, Grenada's neighbors were moved to action by the brutality of the murder of Bishop and many of his followers. Communist efforts to assume control over the island were then abruptly thwarted by the action of the Caribbean Multinational Force.

The Soviet Union's activities in Grenada provided a vivid contrast with its efforts to portray itself as a peaceful power seeking normal diplomatic relations with regional governments. The action of the Caribbean Multinational Force exposed the extent of Soviet and Cuban activities in Grenada and revealed their methods of gaining influence within a country.

Poland

The Soviet Union has employed all available means, including military force, to preserve its hegemony among its satellites in Eastern Europe and elsewhere. In Hungary in 1956, and again in Czechoslovakia in 1968, Soviet troops flagrantly violated the sovereignty of their Allies and suppressed incipient democratic movements.

In Poland, from the rise of the Solidarity Movement in August 1980 to the imposition of martial law in December 1981, the Soviets used the threat of intervention to pressure the Polish Government to suppress the free trade union—an independent, mass movement of some 10 million workers. From the outset, a Soviet psychological warfare campaign against the Polish people began with articles and editorials in the press warning about the

Chapter VII The Global Challenge

consequences of deviating from the socialist path and pointedly describing the fate of Czechoslovakia. Various Soviet leaders accused the Solidarity leadership of being under the influence of foreign powers and of plotting a counterrevolution.

When these threats failed to have the desired results, the Soviets took more direct action. On at least three occasions, they undertook preparations that gave them the option to intervene militarily in Poland. In the fall of 1980, the Soviets mobilized reservists in several Soviet divisions in the Western USSR. At the same time, they increased the readiness of selected forces in Poland, Czechoslovakia and East Germany and summoned to Moscow the commanders of Soviet forces in East Germany and Czechoslovakia.

During the first half of 1981, the Soviets continued to exert political, diplomatic and military pressure on the Polish government. In early March, a public announcement was made of forthcoming Warsaw Pact exercises in Poland and neighboring countries. The announcement could only remind the Polish people that they were vulnerable to "fraternal assistance" if they persisted in supporting "antisocialist" ideas and organizations. During the exercise, Warsaw Pact forces had the opportunity to refine plans for the movement of large formations into and across Poland. Following this show of force, Party Secretary Brezhnev demanded that the Polish Communist Party reassert control over the media and reverse "counterrevolutionary trends."

Soviet options to intervene militarily in Poland were further strengthened during a fall exercise that mobilized Soviet forces in the Baltic Sea and Western Military Districts. The proximity of the exercise conveyed a strong political message to the Polish people by reminding them of the realities of their geographical position, and demonstrated the extent of Soviet military preparedness in the region. More than a year of Soviet threats and intimidation culminated in the imposition of martial law by Polish authorities on December 13, 1981.

Afghanistan

Events over the past half decade in Afghanistan illustrate Soviet willingness to use force when other measures fail. After the 1978 Communist coup in Afghanistan, the Soviets launched a major effort aimed at ensuring their control of the Nur Mohammad Taraki regime. A treaty of friendship and cooperation between the USSR and Afghanistan was signed, and Soviet advisers were assigned to key government institutions. Despite Soviet efforts, however, the new Afghan regime remained weak and was unable to cope effectively with the growing rebellion of various Muslim tribes. In September 1979, the Soviets were involved in a second coup that resulted in the death of Taraki and the installation of Hafizullah Amin as head of the Government of Afghanistan. According to a former KGB officer, the Soviet leadership who had supported Amin in this coup, quickly became disenchanted. In December 1979, the Soviets staged a third coup that resulted in the death of Amin. A new government under long-time Communist Babrak Karmal was installed in Kabul and, at the same time, Soviet military forces invaded Afghanistan.

Today over 108,000 Soviet troops are stationed in Afghanistan. The Karmal regime is alienated from the population and is totally dependent upon Soviet support. Disregarding political and social considerations, the Soviet Union has reverted primarily to the use of force to eliminate opposition. Soviet forces have violated international conventions using lethal chemical agents on Afghan Freedom Fighters and Afghan villages, killing innocent civilians as well as military combatants. Despite the high costs of this involvement, the USSR is apparently committed to a war of attrition against Afghan Freedom Fighters.

Shooting Down of Korean Airliner

In the early morning of September 1, 1983, Soviet fighter aircraft shot down Korean Airlines Flight 007, resulting in the death of all 269 people on board. This unarmed Boeing 747 passenger aircraft was en route from New York to Seoul when it strayed from its established air route and flew over Soviet territory. The aircraft was destroyed apparently without any warning by air-to-air missiles as it was leaving Soviet airspace west of Sakhalin Island.

The belated Soviet explanation for this brutal act sought to deny responsibility for the deaths of the civilian passengers by accusing the United States of using a commercial airliner to conduct a "major intelligence mission" against Soviet military facilities on the Kamchatka Peninsula and Sakhalin Island.

Moscow has further maintained that the Soviet interceptors issued all the proper warnings prior to the destruction of the aircraft. Yet the transcript of the Soviet pilots' communications with their ground controllers clearly contradict this claim. KAL Flight 007 was intercepted and destroyed for having entered Soviet Airspace. The Soviet explanation has not been accepted by either the United Nations or the International Civil Aviation Organization.

The Response

Soviet Military Power 1984 has reported the continuing expansion and improvement of the Soviet Union's military capabilities across the entire range of potential conflict:

- the modernization, increased capabilities and increased survivability of Soviet intercontinental and theater nuclear forces,
- the continuing development of new generations of ICBMs specifically designed to destroy US missile silos and the bases of US manned bomber deterrent forces,
- the continuing deployment of mobile SS-20 LRINF missiles,
- the swift advances in nuclear and conventional cruise missile capabilities,
- the introduction of new land, sea and air weapons systems, and the parallel improvements in combined arms capabilities,
- the continuing modernization and growth of a logistics system designed to sustain Soviet forces in the field for 60 to 90 days,
- the continuing high priority for military research, development and industry, and the exploitation of Western technology, and
- the increasing evidence of Soviet willingness to project and use military power, as reflected in the preceding case studies.

In light of this threat to the United States and its Allies, the challenge is clear. We must maintain military capabilities sufficient to convince the Soviets that the costs of aggression would be far greater than any possible benefit. These capabilities are the cornerstone of our defense policy. US policy toward the Soviet Union, however, is not merely based on deterrence of Soviet aggression. As the United States has stressed, we are firmly committed, as well, to the pursuit of a comprehensive dialogue with the Soviet Union aimed at minimizing the risk of war and solving some of the real problems in our relationship. Reducing arms and ensuring a more stable military balance stand at the top of our agenda.

The United States' strategic and conventional deterrent has been effective in keeping the peace for more than a generation. In the 38 years since World War II—years marked by periods of major tension and crisis—there has been no nuclear conflict. There has been no military conflict between East-West in Europe, nor any direct combat between the forces of the NATO and Warsaw Pact nations in any corner of the globe.

Over the past two decades, the Soviet Union has expanded and modernized its military forces despite US restraint in weapons programs and efforts to achieve meaningful negotiated arms reductions. It is because we recognize the reality of the Soviet threat that we are taking the necessary steps to maintain a truly credible deterrent capability and, thus, to preserve peace and freedom, while continuing to work for significant, equitable and verifiable arms reductions.

We harbor no illusions about the consequences of any nuclear war between ourselves and the Soviet Union. We believe that neither side could win such a war, but this belief alone is not sufficient to assure prevention of a nuclear war or coercion. We seek to maintain a stable strategic deterrent through a range of strategic retaliatory forces—a Triad of land-based ICBMs, submarine-launched ballistic missiles and manned strategic bombers. This combination of retaliatory options is designed to complicate Soviet planning for any execution of a successful attack against all three force components, while at the same time defending against Soviet technological breakthroughs against any single leg of the Triad. In addition to the multiplicity and flexibility provided in the Triad, strategic nuclear deterrence requires an effective command, control and communications system. Our goal, our strategy and our defense programs are designed to ensure that the Soviet leadership understands as well that there can be no winner in a nuclear war and that the West has the confidence to resist Soviet intimidation.

Soviet advances put at risk the elements of

The carrier MINSK, a highly capable unit contributing to Soviet military power.

our retaliatory forces and demand that we improve these elements. We have made the hard decisions required to maintain our nuclear deterrent, and we have begun to redress deficiencies in strategic systems. Our programs introducing the PEACEKEEPER (MX) ICBM, B-1B strategic bomber, TRIDENT II D-5 submarine-launched ballistic missile and upgraded command, control and communications systems to our forces are examples.

In addition to our strategic nuclear forces, the United States maintains nuclear forces in Europe to deter Soviet attacks against our NATO Allies. These forces are linked with our conventional and strategic nuclear forces under a single, coherent policy of deterrence.

Soviet deployment of SS-20 LRINF missiles in recent years, however, has called into question the NATO deterrent posture. The 1979 NATO dual-track decision—deployment of US GLCM and PERSHING II missiles to Europe, while pursuing an equitable, verifiable arms reduction agreement—reaffirms the credibility of NATO's deterrent. In the face of the USSR's unwillingness thus far to negotiate such an agreement, we have initiated deployment of the GLCMs and PERSHING IIs. Nevertheless, we still hope for, and actively seek, resumption of negotiations to reduce or eliminate all US and Soviet LRINF missiles.

Looking to the continuing challenge, we are examining the possibility of a defense against ballistic missiles. The United States has embarked on the analysis required to define a technically feasible research program in this area and to assess implications of defensive technologies for the prevention of nuclear war, the deterrence of aggression and the prospects for arms reductions.

The composition and role of the United States' conventional forces and those of our Allies are defensive in nature to support a defensive policy. We seek no territorial gain and employ our forces only to defend against threats to our interests and security. This policy allows a potential aggressor the advantage of being able to select the time, place and method of any planned attack to maximize his strength and exploit our weaknesses. To compensate for this, the United States must have effective and reliable command, control, communications and intelligence systems and flexible and mobile conventional land, sea and air warfare forces that can respond rapid-

ly and fight effectively in any contingency.

We have undertaken programs to enhance the capabilities of our central command authorities and military force commanders to obtain more extensive and timely information and to communicate effectively with their forces. At the same time, we are improving the readiness of our forces to respond quickly to attack, and we are upgrading Reserve component forces, enabling them to mobilize rapidly and deploy to battle areas early enough to influence a conflict. We are improving force mobility through procurement of airlift and sealift forces, and we are prepositioning equipment and supplies in key theaters to enable rapid response in areas of conflict.

To redress deficiencies in our ability to sustain any conflict, we are investing in munitions, spares and other materiel. We are continuing with programs to modernize our forces with upgraded weaponry to give them a qualitative edge so essential should combat be required against superior numbers. We are expanding the size of selected types of forces, where past neglect has resulted in shortfalls. We are also improving, domestically and internationally, our export control system to halt Soviet exploitation of militarily-significant Western equipment and technology.

The defense programs we and our Allies are pursuing are redressing critical deficiencies in the military balance. These programs are designed to maintain the deterrent element of our defense policy. This task is not an easy one, nor can it be realized over a short period of time. If our deterrent is to remain effective, we and our Allies must maintain a commitment to the completion of these programs and to taking whatever additional steps are necessary to deny the Soviets political advantage through the use or the potential use of their Armed Forces. Only through demonstrated commitment on our part to denying the Soviets such advantage may we hope to bring them to the negotiating table for serious arms reductions. Consistency in our resolve to maintain the security of all free nations is essential if we are to realize the much more desirable goal—greatly reduced levels of armaments of all types in a world at peace.

☆ U.S. GOVERNMENT PRINTING OFFICE 1984-434-463